First World War
and Army of Occupation
War Diary
France, Belgium and Germany

19 DIVISION
Divisional Troops
Divisional Cyclist Company
17 July 1915 - 30 April 1916

WO95/2067/2

The Naval & Military Press Ltd
www.nmarchive.com
Published in association with The National Archives

Published by

The Naval & Military Press Ltd

Unit 10 Ridgewood Industrial Park,

Uckfield, East Sussex,

TN22 5QE England

Tel: +44 (0) 1825 749494

www.naval-military-press.com

www.nmarchive.com

This diary has been reprinted in facsimile from the original. Any imperfections are inevitably reproduced and the quality may fall short of modern type and cartographic standards.

© Crown Copyright
Images reproduced by permission of The National Archives, London, England, 2015.

Contents

Document type	Place/Title	Date From	Date To
Heading	WO95/2067 19 Div Cyclist Coy Jul 1915-Apr 1916		
Heading	19th Division 19th Divl Cyclist Coy. Jly 1915-Apl 1916		
Heading	19th Division 19th Divl: Cyclist Coy: Vol: I Jly Aug & Sept 15		
Heading	War Diary of 19th Division Cyclist Company from 17th July 1915 To 19 Sep 1915 Volume I		
War Diary	Bulford	17/07/1915	17/07/1915
War Diary	Southampton	17/07/1915	17/07/1915
War Diary	Havre	18/07/1915	19/07/1915
War Diary	St Omer	20/07/1915	20/07/1915
War Diary	Serques	20/07/1915	23/07/1915
War Diary	Hazebrouck	23/07/1915	24/07/1915
War Diary	Lillers	24/07/1915	31/07/1915
War Diary	Merville	31/07/1915	31/08/1915
War Diary	Hingette	31/08/1915	19/09/1915
Miscellaneous	Description.		
Miscellaneous	O.C., Divnl. Squadron. O.C., Divnl. Cyclist. G.O.C., 57th Infy Bde. G.O.C., 58th Infy. Bde.	12/08/1915	12/08/1915
Miscellaneous	Instruction for Collection and Disposal of Prisoners of War.	17/09/1915	17/09/1915
Miscellaneous	1st Army.	21/09/1915	21/09/1915
Diagram etc	Markings for Horse Drain and Motor Vehicles		
Operation(al) Order(s)	19th Division Order No. 2.	23/07/1915	23/07/1915
Miscellaneous	1st Army. General Staff. No. G.S. 132 Indian Corps.	28/07/1915	28/07/1915
Miscellaneous	19th Division No. H/2/Z 56th Infantry Brigade.	30/07/1915	30/07/1915
Miscellaneous	Copy of 1st Army No. G.S. 128, dated 27/7/15.	27/07/1915	27/07/1915
Miscellaneous	O.C. Divl. Squadron. Cyclist Coy. G.O.C. R.A. C.R.E. G.O.C. 56th Inf. Bde. G.O.C. 57th Inf. Bde. G.O.C. 58th Inf. Bde. O.C. 5th S. Wales Bordrs. (Pnrs). A.D.M.S. O.C. Divl. Train.	29/07/1915	29/07/1915
Operation(al) Order(s)	19th Division Order No. 5.	30/07/1915	30/07/1915
Miscellaneous	Headquarters, Indian Corps.	01/08/1915	01/08/1915
Heading	Cyclist Coy.	02/08/1915	02/08/1915
Miscellaneous	19th Division No. I.110 H.Q. Indian Corps (Intelligence)	07/08/1915	07/08/1915
Miscellaneous	19th Division. Present Organisation of Defensive Works.		
Miscellaneous	Extract from Centre-Espionage Summary, Part II, 31st July 1915.	03/08/1915	03/08/1915
Miscellaneous	O.C. Divisional Cavalry. O.C. Divisional Cyclist Co. Headquarters 56th Infantry Brigade. Headquarters 57th Infantry Brigade Headquarters 58th Infantry Brigade Headquarters Divisional R.A, C.R.E. O.C. 5th Bn. S. Wales Borders.	15/08/1915	15/08/1915
Miscellaneous	Not to be taken beyond Brigade Headquarters. Tactical Notes. Issued by the General Staff, G.H.Q.	31/07/1915	31/07/1915
Miscellaneous	O.C., Cyclist Coy.	15/08/1915	15/08/1915
Miscellaneous	Headquarters, 56th Infantry Brigade.	02/08/1915	02/08/1915
Miscellaneous	G. A.-1 From Indian Corps to 51st (Highland), Lahore and Meerut Divisions, No G. 139, dated 6-7-15.	06/07/1915	06/07/1915

Miscellaneous	A.A. & Q.M.G. O.C. Divl. Squadron.	17/08/1915	17/08/1915
Miscellaneous	19th Division No. I.201. To.:- All Units.	21/08/1915	21/08/1915
Operation(al) Order(s)	19th Division Order No. 6	26/08/1915	26/08/1915
Miscellaneous	Headquarters, 57th Infantry Brigade. 58th Infantry Brigade.	31/08/1915	31/08/1915
Miscellaneous	O.C. Divisional Cavalry. O.C. Divisional Cyclists.	14/09/1915	14/09/1915
Miscellaneous	Action Of Troops In Reserve.	14/09/1915	14/09/1915
Miscellaneous	H.Q., Lahore Division. H.Q., Meerut Division. H.Q., 19th Division.	14/09/1915	14/09/1915
Miscellaneous	19th Division No. A/1065/L. To All Units.	15/09/1915	15/09/1915
Operation(al) Order(s)	19th Division Order No. 7	12/09/1915	12/09/1915
Miscellaneous	Correction Slip-O.O. No. 8	19/09/1915	19/09/1915
Operation(al) Order(s)	19th Division Order No 8.	19/09/1915	19/09/1915
Miscellaneous	Divl Cyclists Co		
Miscellaneous	Divl. Cyclists	29/09/1915	29/09/1915
Operation(al) Order(s)	19th Division Order No. 10.	28/09/1915	28/09/1915
Heading	19th Division 19th Divl: Cyclist Coy: Vol 2 Sept 15		
Heading	War Diary of 19 Divisional Cyclist Company From 20/9/15 to 26/9/15 Volume II		
War Diary	Hingette	20/09/1915	03/10/1915
Miscellaneous	19th Division Cyclist Company Appendix I	21/09/1915	21/09/1915
Miscellaneous	Revised Instructions Re Accessory.	21/09/1915	21/09/1915
Miscellaneous	19th Division-Instructions.	22/09/1915	22/09/1915
Miscellaneous	19th Division. Artillery arrangements for support of attack.		
Miscellaneous	XIXth Divisional Artillery. Arrangements for support of 2nd Division.		
Miscellaneous	Additions and Amendments to Divisional Order No. 9. Divisional Cyclists	24/09/1915	24/09/1915
Operation(al) Order(s)	19th Division Order No. 9.	22/09/1915	22/09/1915
Miscellaneous	Instructions re Clearing of Battlefield A. No. 3 19th Division. A/63/Z O.C. 19th Div Cyclists	21/09/1915	21/09/1915
Map			
Heading	19th Divl. Cycl. Coy. Vol. 3 Oct 15		
Heading	War Diary of 19th Division Cyclist Company from Oct 4th 1915 to Oct 31st 1915 (Volume 3)		
War Diary	Hingette	01/10/1915	03/10/1915
War Diary	Pacaut	04/10/1915	06/10/1915
War Diary	Zelobes	07/10/1915	14/10/1915
War Diary	Fosse	15/10/1915	20/10/1915
War Diary	Hingette	21/10/1915	31/10/1915
Miscellaneous	O.C. Divl. Cavalry. Divl. Cyclists.	08/10/1915	08/10/1915
Operation(al) Order(s)	19th Division Order No 12.	06/10/1915	06/10/1915
Map	Sketch Map Showing German Units Located on 30.9.15	05/10/1915	05/10/1915
Operation(al) Order(s)	19th Division Order No. 11.	02/10/1915	02/10/1915
Miscellaneous	Addenda to 19th Division Order No. 11.	02/10/1915	02/10/1915
Miscellaneous			
Operation(al) Order(s)	19th Division Order No. 14 Divl Cyclists	19/10/1915	19/10/1915
Miscellaneous	March Table-19th Division.		
Operation(al) Order(s)	19th Division Order No. 13	18/10/1915	18/10/1915
Miscellaneous	March Table-19th Division.		
Miscellaneous	Addendum to 19th Division Order No. 15	22/10/1915	22/10/1915
Operation(al) Order(s)	19th Division Order No. 15	22/10/1915	22/10/1915
Miscellaneous	19th Division No. G.A. 692.	15/10/1915	15/10/1915
Miscellaneous	A Form Messages And Signals.	31/10/1915	31/10/1915

Miscellaneous	1st Army, General Staff, No. G.S. 61. Dated 26/10/15 Adv. 1st Army.	29/10/1915	29/10/1915
Heading	R		
Miscellaneous	Defence Scheme 19th Division, Indian Corps	31/10/1915	31/10/1915
Miscellaneous	Appendix II Instructions Regarding Posts		
Heading	19th Divl. Cycl. Coy. Vol. 4 Nov 15.		
Heading	19th Division Cyclist Coy 1st November to 30th November 1915 Volume IV		
War Diary	Hingette	01/11/1915	08/11/1915
War Diary	Le Casan	09/11/1915	09/11/1915
War Diary	Le Casan (Locon)	10/11/1915	22/11/1915
War Diary	St. Venant	23/11/1915	30/11/1915
Operation(al) Order(s)	19th Division Order No. 16	06/11/1915	06/11/1915
Operation(al) Order(s)	19th Division Order No. 17	15/11/1915	15/11/1915
Operation(al) Order(s)	19th Division Order No. 18	19/11/1915	19/11/1915
Miscellaneous	March Table-19th Division.		
Miscellaneous	Appendix I.		
Miscellaneous	19th Division No. A/574/11 1st Army No. 4/168/A.M.S. 20/10/15.	18/11/1915	18/11/1915
Miscellaneous	I. Alterations in March Table attached to 19th Division Operation Order No. 18 of 19th instant.	20/11/1915	20/11/1915
Heading	19th Divl. Cyclist Vol. 5 Dec 1915		
Heading	War Diary of the 19th Divisional Cyclist Company. from 1st December To 31st December 1915 Volume V		
War Diary	St Venant	01/12/1915	04/12/1915
War Diary	Locon	05/12/1915	31/12/1915
Operation(al) Order(s)	19th Division Order No. 19	03/12/1915	03/12/1915
Miscellaneous	March Table-19th Division.		
Miscellaneous	Addendum to 19th Division Order No. 19	03/12/1915	03/12/1915
Miscellaneous	March Table-19th Division.		
Operation(al) Order(s)	19th Division Order No. 20.	06/12/1915	06/12/1915
Operation(al) Order(s)	19th Division Order No. 21	09/12/1915	09/12/1915
Operation(al) Order(s)	19th Division Order No. 22	17/12/1915	17/12/1915
Miscellaneous	19th Division No. G.A. 106/2. O.C. Divisional Cavalry Cyclists.	16/12/1915	16/12/1915
Operation(al) Order(s)	19th Division Order No. 23	25/12/1915	25/12/1915
Miscellaneous	19th Division No: A/145/Z. Headquarters, 19th Divisional Artillery.	26/12/1915	26/12/1915
Heading	19th Divl. Cyclist Vol: 6		
Heading	War Diary Of 19th Division Cyclist Coy from 1st January to 31st January 1916 Volume VI		
War Diary	Locon	01/01/1916	06/01/1916
War Diary	Trenches (Neuve Chapelle)	06/01/1916	07/01/1916
War Diary	In The Trenches (Neuve Chapelle)	08/01/1916	10/01/1916
War Diary	Les 8 Maisons	10/01/1916	14/01/1916
War Diary	In The Trenches	14/01/1916	19/01/1916
War Diary	Les Huit Maisons	19/01/1916	21/01/1916
War Diary	Locon	21/01/1916	24/01/1916
War Diary	St Venant	25/01/1916	31/01/1916
Heading	19 Div Cycle Coy Vol. 7		
Heading	War Diary of 19th Division Cyclist Coy from 1st to 29th February 1916 Volume VII		
War Diary	St. Venant	01/02/1916	17/02/1916
War Diary	Lestrem	17/02/1916	29/02/1916
Miscellaneous	19. Co		
Miscellaneous	O.C. 19th Division Cyclist Coy.	04/11/1915	04/11/1915

Heading	War Diary of 19th Division Cyclist Company. from 1st to 31st March. 1916 Volume VIII		
War Diary	Lestrem	01/03/1916	02/04/1916
Heading	War Diary of 19th Division Cyclist Coy. from 1st to 30th April 1916 Volume IX		
War Diary	Lestrem	01/04/1916	16/04/1916
War Diary	St. Venant	17/04/1916	18/04/1916
War Diary	Cuhem	19/04/1916	20/04/1916
War Diary	Fressin	21/04/1916	30/04/1916

WO95/2067

10th Div Cyclist Coy

Jul 1915 - April 1916

19TH DIVISION

19TH DIVL CYCLIST COY.
JLY 1915 - APL 1916

TO 3 CORPS

121/6874

19th Division

19th Divl: Cyclist Co.
Vol: I
for Aug. & Sept. 15
apl 16

Army Form C. 2118

WAR DIARY
or
INTELLIGENCE SUMMARY
(Erase heading not required.)

Confidential

War Diary
19. Division Gas Coke Company

From: 17 July 1915 To: 19 Feb 1915

Volume I.

WAR DIARY of the 19th Division Cyclist Co.

or

INTELLIGENCE SUMMARY

Army Form C. 2118

Sheet No. 1

(Erase heading not required.)

Instructions regarding War Diaries and Intelligence Summaries are contained in F. S. Regs., Part II. and the Staff Manual respectively. Title Pages will be prepared in manuscript.

Place	Date	Hour	Summary of Events and Information	Remarks and references to Appendices
BULFORD	17/9/15	1 p.m.	Entrained with Headquarters R.E. 19 Division, for SOUTHAMPTON - Found that 6 ordinary vans were insufficient to carry 232 bicycles, otherwise railway accommodation was sufficient.	JCoel
SOUTHAMPTON	17/9/15	3 p.m.	Arrived at SOUTHAMPTON about 3 p.m. The train was met by the Embarkation Officer. 7 Officers and 193 N.C.O.s and men of this Company went on board the S.S. LA MARGUERITE. 1 Officer and 4 men accompanied the bicycles to transport on the S.S. MATHEREN. The bicycles were stacked on deck. Troops retired to the hotel at dusk and detailed 3 senior officers to take "Submarine" sentries to be myself, 2 Lieutenants being to give warning if approach of 2 hr watches and by means of piece which was in the bivouacks of troops. 2 ~ submarine.	JCpl
HAVRE	18/9/15	5 a.m.	The S.S. MATHEREN anchored off HAVRE at about 5 a.m. and went alongside wharf at 10.30 a.m. The R.M. L.O. came on board. The landing return was not required to be filled. She sailed at Transport. Rations were issued to all troops on board from the S.S. MARGUERITE. A Quartermaster Sergeant. The men and officers start from the boat barges had already disembarked and the Company kindled. Horses and wagons were not given. Transport vehicles were then. These were unstacked & wheeled down gangways. Transport vehicles were then slung ashore by means of gangways. Transport was not clean. I took unit about 3.30 p.m. The Company with the exception of details marching with the transport moved off under the C.O. at about 11.30 a.m. to a guide detailed by the Q.M.L.O. to No.5 Rest Camp.	JCpl
HAVRE	19/9/15	6 a.m.	A party, under an Officer marched to the entraining point LA GARE DES MARCHANDISES & arrived there at 6 a.m. to report to the R.T.O., with the train and then of about 7 men filed down on equipment. The Company formed up in the station yard and bicycles on the trucks. A party had been detailed to the platform & put bicycles on the train. The men note - cattle trucks, 15 & 2nd class carriages arriving.	JCpl

WAR DIARY of 19th Division CYCLIST COY

Army Form C. 2118

Sheet No. 2.

INTELLIGENCE SUMMARY

Place	Date	Hour	Summary of Events and Information	Remarks and references to Appendices
HAVRE (cont'd)	19/7/15		Provided for the Officers. Excellent tea & hot coffee were given to the Men & from H. British Coffee Stall run by voluntary aid. In return for his kind & every Officer, NCO & man drew a full day's ration. In addition to his emergency ration, before entering the train. The entrainment was fully completed a considerable time before the train moved out. Train moved out until nearly 10 a.m.	JCW
ST OMER	20/7/15		Arrived at ST OMER in the morning. Journey lay via JUXIN — ABBEVILLE — BOULOGNE for the men, but the journey which ours via ROUEN — ABBEVILLE — BOULOGNE. General halts were made at length where the toilet & not the general wash of the men & horses could be attended to. The men & horses working arrangement had been got ready at once & on the halts.	JCW
			In detraining the Company fell in in three clear platforms and platforms were marshalled to the siding, a partition was detached to off-load the transport and details, proceeded by route march to SERGUES officers & transport and details, proceeded by route march to SERGUES	JCW
SERGUES	20/7/15		Went into close billets in 3 farms headquarters; officers room, orderly room all at the Mairie. Alarm post = Paint of Helpe	JCW
	21/7/15		Got kit received 50 rounds ammunition per man were issued. Maps HAZEBROUCK S.A. were issued. Officers & NCO's Smoke helmets were issued to all ranks. Interpreter joined.	JCW
	22/7/15 23/7/15		Voluntary romance and rehearsal march made. Interpreter S. HUGUES joined Officially certified of marine, confined to Barrack Regimental office.	JCW
HAZEBROUCK	23/7/15		Went into close billets, together with M.M.G. Section and Pioneer Battalion in a fairly built building known locally as the NEW HOSPITAL, S.W.B.	
	24/7/15		Proceeded by route march to LILLERS at 8 a.m. followed by Transport Relays H.D. Horse East in line — HAZEBROUCK; then by 19 Div. Train A.S.C. H.D. Horse went lame near ST. VENANT. 19 Div. TRAIN A.S.C. exchanged the Lain.	JCW

WAR DIARY of the 19th DIVISION CYCLIST CoY

Army Form C. 2118

INTELLIGENCE SUMMARY

Sheet No. 3.

Place	Date	Hour	Summary of Events and Information	Remarks and references to Appendices
HAZEBROUCK (Contd.)	24/7/15			
LILLERS	29/7/15		Went into close billets. LILLERS — Company billeted in a Cinema and little found. Horses stabled. Bicycles stacked. Weapons parked. Market Square. Hqrs in market square. Mess room — Mess RUE DES PROMENADES. Guard mounted over bicycles and transport. Indication as to billets of field cashier + times for drawing money. 1st Payment of Company.	7 C.Y.S.
	25/7/15			
	26/7/15			
	27/7/15			
	28/7/15			
	29/7/15			
	30/7/15		2nd Payment of Company. Billeting Officer & interpreter proceeded to MERVILLE to arrange billets. Billeting Officer reported — billets arranged 2 Company. Proceeded to MERVILLE by route march. Preceded by officer 1/c transport and details. Went into close billets at front. K.34.F.26. (MERVILLE FRANCE. Sheet 36.a.) Company occupied a workshop shed. Bicycles stacked and waggons parked — adjoining field. Guard mounted.	7 C.Y.S.
	31/7/15			
MERVILLE	1/8/15 to 6/8/15		Quiet in training of E. Company. Route marches. Field Days. Practice — Containing & Developing centre of guard. 1st payment 6/8/15	
			Company fully satisfied 6/8/15 and furnished D.H.Q. Guard and a fatigue Party. Cooks Course 2 N.C.O.'s & 2 men. Unity to follow hunger does not favour firing. Orders given by Platoon Commanders particularly were their men against drinking unsterilised or non-sterilised water.	7 C.Y.S.
	7/8/15 9/8/15		Quiet in training. On 9/8/15 4/14 P.C.S. FIELDS-CLARKE proceeded to ENGLAND on Transfer to R.E. Received copy of Mob. Orn. Till acted as July 20/9/15 showing addition to Establishment of 1. Cook Sht. 1 Draught Horse and 1 Private.	7 C.Y.S.
	14/8/15 20/8/15		Quiet in training & practice of 5 acts on Trench Guides. 1st payment of Company 4/8/15. On 20/8/15 6 NCOs were posted to 8.H.Q. of Company on 20/8/15.	7 C.Y.S.

WAR DIARY of the 19th DIVISION CYCLIST Coy

INTELLIGENCE SUMMARY

Sheet No. 4

Place	Date	Hour	Summary of Events and Information	Remarks and references to Appendices
MERVILLE (cont)	30/8/15		Carried on with the training of the Company. 6th Fragment of the Company on 27/8/15. Lieut J.T. MOILLIET and 50 N.C.O's & men commenced work on the 19 Division Salvage Company under instructions from B.H.Q. The Company was formed to salve arms, ammunition, equipment etc, left by troops in the area. The firing line. The supervision of the Company is in the hands of Capt. FROST Officer i/c Trench Tramways INDIAN CORPS Salvage Coy. H.Q. in charge No S.T.C. centre (Not BETHUNE. Continued sheet 36.a, 26.c, 36, 36.c.)	
	31/8/15		On 31/8/15 furnished the various Guards furnished by the Company and dropped links were relieved. Each guard consists of 1 N.C.O. 3 men. Returns were delivered to the first motor cars by means of motor car transfer, but afterwards men carried them on return full etc. on their bicycles. The Guards were visited daily by the Orderly Officer and fragments of the Coy. Bn 3/8/15 proceeded by motorbike to front W.11.6.27. (Ref. 36.A.)	7 cars 7 cars
HINGETTE	31/8/15		Went into close billets in 3 farms about front W.11.6.27 (Ref. 36.A.) Bicycles stashed and wagon parked in centre.	
	4/9/15		Carried on with training of the Company. On 4/9/15 Company commenced work in conjunction with the 19 Division Cavalry to enlarge the main ditches draining the front area. The bicycles were removed from this unit. The Division + was not replaced. The Regiment Company on 7/9/15	7 cyclists 1 R.E.
	10/9/15		Carried on with training & work of Company. On 10/9/15 M.O. M. and reported 2 men suffering from various throats, carroll by drinking well & canal water. This Company has orders to cut off the establishment and supply & told D. hold into twenty difficult weather. Intense sunshine, cloudless most mornings. Evenings short easterly wind weather on 10/9/15 Salvage Co. sent	7.8cars
	11/9/15			
	12/9/15		19th Regiment of Company	7 cars

WAR DIARY of the 19th Division Cyclist Co. Army Form C. 2118
or
INTELLIGENCE SUMMARY

Sheet No. 5

(Erase heading not required.)

Place	Date	Hour	Summary of Events and Information	Remarks and references to Appendices
HINGETTE (CONT)	13/9/15		D.H.Q. guard furnished by this unit & returned by D.H.Q. Also furnished guards 1 NCO and 6 men on 3 bridges and 1 NCO and 3 men regulating traffic - also made Divnl. 1 Tipperary here from 19 Divn. Cycl. Co. complete. Establishment of horses.	7 O.R.s
	14/9/15		Change - weather. Cloudy. Rain.	7 O.R.s
	15/9/15		D.H.Q. guard relieved.	7 O.R.s
	17/9/15		Salvage company formed from this unit, disbanded & weather fine & dry.	7 O.R.s
	18/9/15		Weather fine & dry. Strong Easterly wind.	7 O.R.s
	19/9/15		2/Lt. Talbot joined for duty to replace 2/Lt. R. Fields Clarke transferred to R.E. 3/8/15. Weather fine & dry. Strong Easterly wind. Received copy of M. Division orders No. 8 copy No. 15 dated 19/9/15 re forthcoming operations.	7 O.R.s

Merbert Smith CAPT
O.C. 19th Div. Cyclist Co.

Date	letter number	K or R	Description
23.7.15	D.O. No 2	R.	March Table.
28.7.15	G.A.28	R	Hints on German gas shells.
29.7.15	G.A.33	R.	Information to be given when reporting passage of hostile airship.
30.7.15	A/2/2	R	Report on mounting inspection & relief of sentries asked for.
29.7.15	G.A.17	R.	Moving of the Division.
30.7.15	D.O. No 5	R	March Table
2.8.15	G/4/2	R.	All gold should be changed at Field Cashiers
3.8.15	I.63	R.	Small balloons found believed to have been used for signalling purposes.
8.8.15	I.110	R.	Returns to be rendered showing number of boys who, being fed by British Units are suspects.
	A.6.	R.	Work to be done on the defences.
12.8.15	G.A.52.	K	List of posts to be guarded by Div in Reserve.
14.8.15	G.A.22	K	Memorandum. Notes on Gas.
"	G.A.54	K.	Gas Signals 1st Corps.
15.8.15	G.A.44	R.	Tactical notes Issued by G.S. G.H.Q.
"	G.A.27	R	Various rocket signals
17.8.15	G.A.53	R.	Divisions of I.A.C. front.
21.8.15	I.201	R.	Persons acting in a suspicious manner to be detained for examination
26.8.15	D.O. No 6	R.	19th Div to take over the line from 2nd & 7th Div's.
31.8.15	G.A.60	R.	Work to be done on the defences.
14.9.15	G.A.52	R.	Extracts from Div. Defence Scheme.
15.9.15	A/1065/L	R	No soldier to appear in French Court without instructions from D.H.Q.
19.9.15	I.475	K.	No airships to be fired on except by officers orders a French dirigibles will give a signal.
17.9.15		K	Instructions for Collection & Disposal of prisoners of war.

Date	Letter Number	K or R	Description
12.9.15	D.O.7	R.	Brigade relief.
19.9.15	D.O.8	R.	Readjustment of Front.
28.9.15	D.O.10	R.	Readjustment of Divsnl Front & Relief of Brigade
28.9.15	S/1294	K.	Signs for vehicles instead of 10th Divsn. etc. list of
22.9.15	D.O.9	R.	Orders for an attack.

S E C R E T.
****

No. G.A. 52.

TO :-
   O.C., Divnl. Squadron.
   "   "   Cyclists.
   G.O.C., 57th Infy. Bde.
   "   58th   "   "

****

       The Division, being in reserve, has been charged with the guarding and upkeep of the posts in the "BOUT DEVILLE" area, which is the rearward portion of the areas allotted to the two Divisions in front line.

2.   The guards for each post will consist of 1 N.C.O. and 3 men, and the following list gives the posts which at present have to be guarded, and the source from which guards will be furnished :-

GUARDS FROM.	NAME OF POST.	SQUARE.
57th Brigade.	CEMETERY RIGHT.	L 34 d 4.3.
Divnl. Squadron.	MUDDY LANE.	G 33 c 4.1.
	LE DRUMEZ.	M 2 b.
	CARTER'S.	M 2 c 9.1.
	CLIFTON NORTH.	R 18 a 4.10.
58th Brigade.	PONT RIQUEUL.	R 10 a)
		R 9 b.)
	LESTREM.	R 9 c 2.1.
	LE MARAIS.	(1) R 16 a.
	"	(2) R 16 b.
	"	(3) R 17 a.
	"	(4) R 10 d.
Divnl. Cyclists.	CLIFTON CENTRAL.	R 18 c 8.2.
	" SOUTH.	R 18 c 4.7.
	BOUT DEVILLE NORTH.	R 24 a 6.8.
	VIELLE CHAPELLE X ROADS.	R 28 d 7.6.
	ZELOBES.	R 27 c 1.7.

3.   Please send out at once to reconnoitre the position of the posts allotted to you, so that the necessary guards may proceed there at 10-0 a.m. tomorrow, 13th inst. They will be relieved every 24 hours.

                                                                                                                [signature]

H.Q. 19th Division,   Lieut.Colonel,
12th August 1915.   General Staff.

MEMORANDUM.

INSTRUCTIONS for COLLECTION and DISPOSAL of PRISONERS of WAR.

H.Q. 19th Division.

17th September 1915.

1. During active operations the 19th Divisional Collecting Station will be established at the junction of the LE TOURET road with the RUE DU BOIS road, X. 16.d.4.8., where prisoners will be taken over from the fighting troops by escorts provided under Divisional arrangements.

2. From the advanced collecting station, prisoners, when their numbers are small, will be sent to the Corps Collecting Station at FOSSE where they will be taken over by the Corps.
   In the event of a large number of prisoners, fifty or more being captured, they will be sent to D.H.Q., LOCON and detained there while arrangements are made by the Corps for their evacuation by Divisional Staff. The capture of prisoners will be reported to the A.P.M., Indian Corps, either by wire or by messenger.

3. Men making prisoners will take them to the nearest officer available when they will be searched for explosives or reversed bullets; if these are found on them they will be dealt with on the spot: the remainder will be taken under escort to the advanced Collecting Station at LE TOURET.

4. Escorts will be provided by the fighting troops in the proportion of 15 to 20 per cent of Escort to prisoners – as far as the Divisional Collecting Station, where the A.P.M., 19th Division will take over the prisoners. The fighting troops will then return to the Front. Batches of 100 prisoners, which number should not be exceeded, will be placed under command of an Officer. Unfit prisoners will be taken to the nearest Dressing Station.

5. The route by which escorts are to move from the Divisional Collecting Station to the Corps Station is via LE TOURET, LA COUTRE, FOSSE.
   In order to prevent delay it is important that this route should be adhered to, but if it is found necessary to alter it a message should be at once sent in to the Intelligence Officer at the Corps Collecting Station.

6. The Officer in charge of the Advanced Station will arrange that the first prisoners taken are sent in at once to the Corps Station. After this prisoners may be sent in in suitable batches according to the rate at which they arrive and the escort available. They will be taken over at the Corps Collecting Station by a guard detailed under Corps arrangements.

7. Maps, papers, documents, etc., should be taken off prisoners as early as possible and sent in with each batch, but other articles should be left in their possession as they will be searched at the Corps Collecting Station.
   Before wounded prisoners are handed over to the Medical authorities, all documents should be taken from them.

8. Officers should be separated from other ranks as soon as possible after capture.
   All papers, maps and documents taken from Officers are to be put up into separate bundles and not mixed up with those taken from other ranks.

P.T.O.

9. Officers and N.C.O's in charge of prisoners should have the following precautions fully impressed upon them:-
    (a). Prisoners should be counted,
    (b). Escort should be divided and placed in front and rear with flanks lightly guarded.
    (c). A slow pace only will be set.
    (d). No conversation allowed.
    (e). Prisoners must not be allowed to straggle.
    (f). Prisoners must be halted at some distance from any civilians.
    (g). Prisoners attempting to escape will be shot.
    (h). A receipt should be obtained for all prisoners handed over.

10. Brigades taking prisoners will at once inform Divisional H.Q. General Staff, for information of Indian Corps Intelligence, of the number of prisoners taken and route being sent to Divisional Collecting Station.

11. The Senior Supply Officer will arrange to hold 300 preserved meat and biscuit rations on hand at LOCON for issue to prisoners if required.

P.M.Davies, Lieut-Col.

A.A. & Q.M.G., 19th Division.

G/3498.

1st Army.

In order to lessen as far as possible the information which can be gained by the enemy's agents from the numbering and lettering of vehicles of different formations it has been decided that all letters and the numerals on the outside of vehicles of the principal Units and formations which in any way indicate the formations to which they belong are to be obliterated.

"A" There is no objection to the Units having for their own convenience certain signs or figures in an inconspicuous position provided they in no way indicate the number or ~~the title of Unit~~ 5/et or formation to which unit belongs.

In lieu of titles and numbers the signs shewn in attached paper have been approved to distinguish different classes of transport and will be painted on both sides of all horse drawn and mechanical vehicles other than motor cars of the Units to which they refer.

The W.D. numbers of motor cars and motor lorries are to remain as at present via G.R.O. No 944 dated 21st June 1915.

G.H.Q. ((sd) C.T.Dawkins Major-General.
21.9.15. for Quarter Master General.

Camp Commandant D.H.Q. 19th Divl R.E.
H.Q. 19th Divl Artillery. 19th Divl Train
56th Infantry Brigade A.D.M.S.
57th   do 19th Divl Cyclists
58th   do

Headquarters 19th Division. G/296/L
Forwarded for necessary action.

The letters and numerals should be obliterated and the appropriated symbol painted on either side of all vehicles belonging to 1st Line Transport.

Please see para "A" above. This should be carried out under Brigade arrangements and the proposed identification mark forwarded to D.H.Q. for information and approval.

Indents for paint should be sent to D.A.D.O.S. 19th Divn if it is found impossible to obtain it locally. All baggage and supply wagons will be painted by 19th Divl Train.

Capt. D.A.Q.M.G.
28.9.15. 19th Division.

MARKS FOR HORSE DRAWN AND MOTOR VEHICLES

Brigade Ammunition Column	Divisional Train Supply	Divisional Sub-Park or M.T. Echelon of Ammunition Col.	
Divisional Ammunition Column	Signals R.E.	Army Artillery Park	
1st Line Transport	Field Companies and Field Squadrons R.E.	G. H. Q. Park	
Divisional Train Baggage	Supply Columns	Ammunition Column of R.G.A. Brigades.	

R

19th Division Order No. 2.　　　Copy No. 8

23rd July 1915.

Intention.	1.	The Division will march tomorrow, in accordance with the attached March Table, to the area HAVERSKERQUE — ST VENANT — BUSNES (all exclusive) — LILLERS — BOURECQ — ST HILAIRE — NORRENT FONTES — LAMBRES (all inclusive) — AIRE (exclusive) THIENNES (inclusive).
Long Halt.	2.	The Division will halt from 10-30 a.m. till 12 noon.
Refilling Points.	3.	Refilling will not take place tomorrow.
Reports.	4.	Up till 10-30 a.m. at CHATEAU 1 mile E of EBBLINGHAM STA.; after that time to Chateau at S end of NORRENT FONTES.

Issued at 7-30 p.m.

A.S.Buckle, Lieut-Colonel,
General Staff.

SECRET. G.A.33.

1st Army,
General Staff.
No.G.S.132.
28th July 1915.

Indian Corps.

With a view to ascertaining further details as to modifications in the design of hostile airships and signals employed by their crews, it is desirable that every unit reporting the passage of a hostile airship should furnish also the following information:-

    (a) Name of individual who saw the airship.
    (b) Its general appearance.
    (c) Its estimated height and speed.
    (d) Whether any noise of engines was heard.
    (e) Whether any signal lights were fired.

The telegraphic report is not to be delayed for the inclusion of this information; which should be transmitted by letter to the nearest Squadron R.F.C. with least possible delay.

                        (sd) R.Butler. Major-General.
28th July 1915.   General Staff, 1st Army.

==========

OC Divisional Cyclists Co.

For information. *Please acknowledge*
receipt. *Acknowledged sent*

H.Q.19th Division.   Major.
29/7/15.   General Staff.

Confidential.

19th Division No. A/2/2

56th Infantry Brigade.
57th   -do-
58th   -do-
19th R.A.
19th R.E.
19th Divl. Train.
19th Supply Column.
19th Divl. Cavalry.
19th Divl. Cyclist Coy.
19th Signal Coy.
19th Divl. Ammunition Column.
Camp Commandant, D.H.Q. Unit.
A.D.M.S., 19th Division.
Motor Machine Gun Battery.
31st Mobile Veterinary Section.
Cable Section.

Copy of 1st Army G.S. 128 dated 27/7/15, overleaf, is forwarded for information and communication to all concerned.
Please report for the information of the Major-General Commanding the general method adopted for the mounting of sentries, their inspection and relief.

Lieut-Colonel,
A.A. & Q.M.G., 19th Division.

D.H.Q.
30/7/15.

CONFIDENTIAL.

Copy of 1st Army No. G.S. 128, dated 27/7/15.

The number of cases of men being tried by Court Martial for sleeping on their post is large, and the figures show that this form of crime is greatly on the increase.

The number of such cases in the 1st Army in May was 9, in June 20, and for the first three weeks in July 35.

From an investigation of these cases it appears that the majority are due to the men being tired out when they are mounted either from having been employed on some strenuous work during the day, or from having taken no rest during the day after having been on fatigue, etc., throughout the previous night.

It is recognised that at times, as for instance when fighting is in progress, it may be unavoidable to mount as sentries men who are tired, but in such cases reliefs should be more frequent and constant inspection is necessary. In normal times no such difficulties should arise, and the large increase in the number of sentries who are found asleep on their posts seems to point to a want of method in detailing reliefs and to a lack of supervision of the men on the part of Company Officers.

The G.O.C. directs that this matter should receive your attention, and that the method of mounting sentries, their inspection and relief should be enquired into.

SECRET.

O.C. Divl.Squadron.
　　　Cyclist Coy.
G.O.C. R.A.
C.R.E.
G.O.C. 56th Inf.Bde.
　"　　57th　"　"
　"　　58th　"　"
O.C. 5th S.Wales Bordrs. (Pnrs).
A.D.M.S.
O.C. Divl.Train.

Reference to 1/40,000 Map)

       The Divisions is about to move into an area round MERVILLE, in Corps Reserve.

2.   The LAHORE and MEERUT Divisions are being reorganized and will divide the front of the line held by the Corps, LAHORE Division on the right. The front will extend from about Square N.13.a to Square S.9.d, the dividing line between the Divisions being roughly Square M.35.--- Rouge CROIX --- PONT ROCHON; headquarters LAHORE Division LESTREM, of MEERUT Division LE N'AU MONDE (Square G.33.a)

3.   The above arrangements are to be completed by 6 am on 2nd August. On a date after 2nd August to be arranged later, the 56th Infy.Bde. and 81st Fld.Coy.R.E. will be attached for about 8 days to LAHORE Division, and the 57th Infy.Bde. and 82nd Fld.Coy.R.E. to the MEERUT Division, for further training in the special form of warfare now obtaining, including further instruction in the use of hand grenades and trench mortars. To each Division will also be attached for instruction during the same time 1 troop of the Divl.Squadron and 1 Coy. 5/S.W.B.

4.   During this attachment each man will be in the trenches for at least 48 hours. Two battalions will probably be attached from each of the two Infantry Brigades at a time.

5.   When the above troops have completed their period of instruction, the 58th Brigade will be instructed in its turn, probably two battalions with each of the Indian Divisions, together with the Cyclist Coy. and the remainder of the 5/S.W.B. and Divl.Squadron.

6.   The B.G.R.A., Indian Corps, is about to make arrangements for the attachment of Artillery Commanders and Staffs and Artillery Units for short periods to the Indian Divisions in the same way as above.

7.   The D.D.M.S., Indian Corps, is about to take similar action with regard to medical personnel.

8.   In addition to the above attachments arrangements have been made for facilities to be afforded by the G.Os.C Indian Divisions to Commanders and Staffs of this Division for becoming acquainted with the first line and the defences in rear of it.

H.Q. 19th Division.

29/7/15.

Lieut-Colonel.
General Staff.

Copy No. 15

19th Division Order No.5.
****

30th July 1915.

Moves. 1. The Division, less 56th Brigade Group and Divl. Squadron, moving there to-day, will move to Corps Reserve Area in accordance with the attached March Table.

Supply. 2. Refilling Points:-   (refilling 9-30 am)

    56th Brigade Group   )   MEURILLON (L.31)
    57th Brigade Group   )
      less 87th Bde.R.F.A.)   "
    Divl.Squadron.   "
    Divl.Ammn.Col.   As at present.
    Remainder of Divn.   HAM-EN-ARTOIS.

Reports. 3. Reports, up till 2-0 pm tomorrow, to BUSNES Chateau, after 2-0 pm to MERVILLE, K.29.d.8.3.

Issued at 2-45 pm

A.S.Buckle. Lieut-Colonel.
General Staff.

CONFIDENTIAL.
Headquarters, Indian Corps.
Dated the 1st August 1915.

Copy of a letter No.Q/C/48, dated 30th July 1915, from the Quarter Master General, General Headquarters, to 1st Army.

The Field Marshal Commanding-in-Chief wishes to impress upon all ranks in the British Expeditionary Force the extreme importance at this juncture of their surrendering any British Gold coinage which may be in their possession in exchange for French currency, as advantage may accrue to the enemy by reason of British gold coming into their possession either through Agents or by direct appropriation from dead or captured soldiers.

The Generalissimo of the French Army, General Joffre, has already addressed a similar letter to that Army, in which he has informed them that Germany is sparing no effort to increase her stock of gold by every means in her power.

Arrangements are being made through the medium of the Field and Base Cashiers and of the Army Post Offices throughout France for exchanging gold in possession of officers and soldiers, and the Commander-in-Chief desires that you will explain to all ranks under your Command the necessity of their availing themselves of the opportunities afforded for exchanging their gold.

From 1st Army, to Indian Corps, No.C/260, dated 30-7-15.

For necessary action.

III.

No.61/I/Q.

For necessary action.

A.W. Peck,
Lieut-Colonel,
A.Q.M.G.
Indian Corps.

TO:- H.Q. Lahore Divn.
" Meerut Divn.
" 19th Division.
" No.1 Group H.A.R.
O.C. 4th Brigade R.G.A.
" Ind: Corps Ammn: Park.
" No.18 Sec: Anti Aircraft Guns.
" No.5 M.M.G. Batty.
" Dett: 3-Pdr Hotchkiss Batty.
" Lahore Supply Column.
" Meerut Supply Column.
" 19th Divl. Supply Column.
" Ind: Corps Troops Supply Col.
" Corps Hqrs. Signal Coy.
" Camp Commandant.

Confidential.

Cyclist Coy.

For information and guidance

A.J. Farrar Major
for DAA & QMG
19th Division

D.H.Q.
2/8/15.

Confidential.

For Reply see
6.12

COPY.   SECRET   19th Division No. I.110.

                                       1st Army No.145 (I.1)

H.Q. Indian Corps
     (Intelligence)

    The Secret Service report that in a certain number of British units boys and young men, below military age, who pretend to be refugees, are being fed and are allowed to remain in the billets of the unit.

    It is reported from other sources that in certain cases these children are German Agents. Please submit a list of all children who are with units so that they may be examined by the Secret Service.

7/8/15.   (sd) J.Charteris   Major.
                                    General Staff, 1st Army.

H.Q. 19th Division.
 "   Lahore Division.
 "   Meerut Division.

    No. I.G. 512.   7th August 1915.

    Forwarded for information.

    The lists required by 1st Army should be submitted to Corps Headquarters with the least possible delay.

    If there are no names, a blank return should be rendered.

Indian Corps.   (sd) W.L.D.Twiss. Captain.
                                    General Staff.

To:-

O.C. Divisional Cyclist Co.

    For report please, by 12 noon, on the 9th instant.

                                    [signature]
                                              Major.
H.Q. 19th Division.   General Staff.
8/8/15.

SECRET.

19th Division.
Present Organization of Defensive Works.

(1). The infantry occupying the trenches will concentrate on the thickening and raising of the parapet of the fire-trench, on preparation of cover therein, and on digging communication trenches thence to the support line; the latter work will be done in conjunction with the Pioneers.

One Field Company R.E. will be allotted to each Section of the line; the Brigade Commander being always able to call on its C.O. for advice and supervision of work, and also for the services of one Section of the Company if necessary.

(2) Two Companies of the Pioneer Battalion will be detailed to each Section for work on support trenches and on the communication trenches between fire and support trenches (and (under the C.R.E.)

(3). (a) The remainder of the two Field Companies R.E. allotted to Sections of the line, not employed as in (1) above, will be under the direct orders of the C.R.E. for work in forward lines.

(b) The third Field Company will be similarly employed on back lines.

(4). One battalion of the Reserve Brigade will be employed, under the C.R.E., on the improvement of communication trenches from the support trenches to the rear. Half the battalion will work in each Section. The object to be aimed at is to get 4 communication trenches in each Section which will really provide cover. They will be -

Left Section.	Right Section.
SHETLAND ROAD	GRENADIER ROAD.
ROPE TRENCH.	BARNETON ROAD.
FUSHEL TRENCH.	LOTHIAN ROAD.
CADBURY TRENCH.	PIONEER ROAD.

(5). The Divisional Cavalry and Cyclists will work at the improvement of the main ditches draining the area.

A.Butler

SECRET.

Extract from CONTRE-ESPIONAGE SUMMARY, Part II,
31st July 1915.

1. Several small balloons have been found, deflated, lying on the ground. They are about 14 inches long by 8 inches wide when in the deflated state, and contain a small electric lamp, which is about the size of that used in a small electric torch. The exact use of these balloons has not yet been discovered. The French Authorities consider that they are used in a system of direct signalling.

No. I.63.

Headquarters,
    Divnl. R.A.
    56th Infy. Bde.
    57th   "   "
    58th   "   "
    C.R.E.
    5/S.W.Borderers.
    Divnl. Squadron.
    Cyclist Coy.
    Signal Coy.
    A.P.M.

    Any information should be forwarded to D.H.Q. as soon as possible.

                                          Mackenzie

H.Q.19th Divn.,
3rd August 1915.
                                            Major, G.S.,
                                            19th Division.

SECRET.   G.A.44.

O.C. Divisional Cavalry.
  ,,   ,,   Cyclist Co.
Headquarters 56th Infantry Brigade.
      ,,   57th   ,,   ,,
      ,,   58th   ,,   ,,
      ,,   Divisional R.A.
C.R.E.
O.C. 5th Bn. S. Wales Borderers.

Herewith 1 copy of General Staff pamphlet No.50 entitled "TACTICAL NOTES" for your information. Please acknowledge receipt.

H.Q. 19th Division,
15th August 1915.

Major, G.S.,
19th Division.

CONFIDENTIAL.

Not to be taken beyond Brigade Headquarters.

O.B./39.

Tactical Notes.

Issued by the General Staff, G.H.Q.

---

1. The following notes have been compiled from reports received from formations which have taken part in recent operations:—

They contain information with regard to—(i.) the maintenance of communication with the Infantry after it has advanced to the assault; (ii.) methods for dealing with hostile machine guns; (iii.) methods of indicating points reached by our attacking troops; (iv.) methods for reinforcing the front line; (v.) some miscellaneous questions.

Maintenance of Communication with the Infantry after it has advanced to the assault.

Telephones.

2. Between the front line trenches and Divisional and Brigade Headquarters telephone lines must be in triplicate, or even in quadruplicate, and one line should be buried; "ladders" at frequent intervals are also necessary.

Beyond the "departure" trench, it has been found possible to run out telephone lines. They are either taken forward with the first advancing troops, or are run out quickly during pauses in the enemy's fire; but they are liable to constant damage by hostile artillery.

The telephone cannot, therefore, be relied on after the Infantry has advanced. It has, however, so many advantages over other means of communication that every effort should be made to lay the lines and keep them in repair.

Other methods for maintaining communication are given below.

Orderlies.

3. This form of communication is the most used, and though it is slow and requires a considerable expenditure of personnel, it has proved in the end to be the most reliable.

In some formations, officers have been used for this purpose. One officer is detailed by each Battalion and is charged with the duty of maintaining communication between Brigade Headquarters and his unit; he should be accompanied by an orderly.

It may sometimes be possible for these officers to transmit information back to Brigade Headquarters, after they have reached their unit, by means of the telephone used by the Artillery forward observing officers.

More generally, however, "runners" have been used, each message being sent by at least two independent "runners." The men are specially selected; a suitable distribution is 4 per Company with 6 at Battalion Headquarters. "Runners" have also been used to form a chain of communicating files along a marked feature (trench, hedge, pathway, etc.), messages being passed along the chain.

It is most important to connect our line by some sort of communicating trench with the enemy's front line as soon as the latter has been captured. Even if this is only a foot or two deep, orderlies can crawl to and fro. Parties should be told off to continue the saps previously run out towards the enemy's line as soon as the assault is delivered, and other parties should also be told off to work backwards from the captured trench to meet them.

Visual Signalling.

4. Semaphore, Dietz discs, lamps, helio and flag have all been used at various times. The great difficulty has been to avoid observation by the enemy, especially in flat country, though this can sometimes be overcome by the use of ruined houses, haystacks, trees, etc.

Good results have been obtained from visual signalling in the more advanced portions of the line by sending from front to rear only, each message being repeated three times without acknowledgement or reply from the receiving station.

The Siemens' improved electric signalling lamp has on the whole proved the most efficacious apparatus for the above purpose both by day and by night.

Method of dealing with Hostile Machine Guns.

5. The difficulties are:—
    (i.) How to locate the guns.
    (ii.) How to dispose of them when located.

German machine guns are often placed in one of the following positions:—
    (a) In a very thick advanced traverse, firing so as to flank the main parapet.
    (b) At a trench junction.
    (c) Dug in, very low in the parapet itself.
    (d) In cellars.
    (e) Dug in, in front of ruined houses.

The difficulty of locating guns in such positions is obvious, nor is it easy to draw their fire beforehand as they are often kept hidden, and only moved up into position when an attack is imminent.

6. Careful and continuous observation is the best means of locating the emplacements. A heavy bombardment on the first line and support trenches, both on the front of attack and on the flanks, appears to offer the best chance of destroying the guns: while a barrage of H.E. shell on both flanks of the Infantry attack, directed on the enemy's trenches and tactical points in rear will probably neutralise their fire.

The following methods of dealing with them have also been found successful at different times :—

(a) By rifle or machine gun fire concentrated on the emplacement, if it has been located. This is reported to be quicker and more effective than shrapnel.

(b) By trench mortars and rifle grenades, fire being concentrated on likely places. In one instance 14 trench mortars were concentrated against suspected machine gun positions and none came into action in that part of the line.

Method of indicating positions reached by our troops.

7. The following methods have been used *by day* :—

(a) Coloured screens about 3 feet by 2 feet, on two poles 4 feet 6 inches long, the side facing the enemy being covered with inconspicuous green material. These were found of great value to the Artillery observing officers.

(b) Flags or discs on 9 or 10 ft. poles. These poles were unnecessarily long and cumbersome.

(c) Sides of biscuit tins placed behind the trenches or houses captured by our troops so as to be visible from the rear.

(d) Strips of white material laid down on the ground for identification by aircraft. Unless some such method is employed aircraft cannot distinguish between our own and the enemy's troops.

The drawbacks to all the above are that if the position has to be evacuated the signal may be left behind and so become misleading; moreover, if captured, it discloses our arrangements to the enemy. The design of the screen, flag, or disc, also must be changed on each occasion.

(e) Placing caps on rifles and holding them above the trench. This has been very generally used.

(f) Daylight fireworks. These are reported to have been effective.

By night :—

(g) Coloured rockets and Very's pistol lights, the colours or combination of colours being changed for each operation.

The Germans, however, are in the habit of sending up rockets as soon as an attack starts in order to create confusion.

Movement of supports to reinforce the front line.

8. It has been found that troops detailed for the assault must be formed in considerable depth, and that trenches with good splinter proof cover are necessary for this assembly. These trenches should be prepared in successive lines according to the cover from view obtainable. A suitable distance between lines has been found to be from 40 to 50 yards.

Plenty of efficient communication trenches must be dug to connect these lines from front to rear at intervals of not more than 50 or 60 yards apart, so that troops may move up to the front with the least possible loss and delay.

Communication trenches must be told off as "up" and "down" trenches and picketed to ensure that they are only used in one direction only.

Sidings off these trenches are essential.

At intervals there should be communication trenches wide enough to admit of the evacuation of wounded men.

Any attempt to crowd troops into a confined space, in immediate proximity to the front line leads to heavier casualties than an advance from lines in rear.

Experience has shown that once an attack is checked it is seldom helped forward by supporting troops pushed up directly behind it. The desired result is more likely to be obtained by pushing on on the flanks of the troops which have been checked, or else by a bombardment of the hostile positions in front of them.

9. **The following points are also brought to notice :—**

(a) Our own wire can be removed during the period of heavy bombardment; it must have been previously prepared the night before. It is advisable that the removal of the wire should take place as late as possible, in order that the enemy may not receive warning of the impending attack.

(b) Artillery barrages should be directed on to the enemy's supporting points and communications, and not on open spaces of ground which leads to waste of ammunition.

Should the enemy be seen to start forming up to deliver counter attacks it is desirable to allow him to do so; once formed up he can be heavily punished.

(c) Reports have been received that the flashing of bayonets over the tops of forming up trenches or parapets discloses the position of the Infantry assembled to attack. This should be guarded against.

(d) The organisation of grenadier parties, particularly as regards the bringing up of reserves of grenades as the attack progresses is most important.

(e) Above all, it is important to vary the methods employed each time an attack is delivered. This applies particularly to artillery bombardments.

G.H.Q.,
31st July, 1915.

[O.B./50.]

S E C R E T.   G.A.27.

My G.A.27 of 2/8/15 is amended as follows:-

(i) Signals (a) Enemy infantry attacking.
         (b) Heavy artillery or trench mortar bombardment of our trenches.

In both cases the two rockets will be repeated after a half-minute interval instead of a two minute interval.

(ii) The following signal is added:-
         (c) "Our own shells falling short; lengthen range".

Two red rockets sent up and repeated in a similar manner to signals (a) and (b).

H.Q. 19th Divn.
15/8/15.

                                Major.
                          General Staff.

S E C R E T.   G.A.27.

Headquarters,
        56th Infantry Brigade.
        57th   "   "
        58th   "   "
Officer Commndg. 5th S.Wales Borderers.
C.R.A.
C.R.E.
O.C. Divl. Cavalry.
O.C. Divl. Cyclist Company. ✓
  "   Divl. Signal Company.
  "   Divl. Train.
  "   M.M.G. Battery.

          The attached is forwarded for your information, please. *(1 Copy) Please acknowledge receipt.*

H.Q.19th Division,
2/8/15.
                              Major.
                            General Staff.

Secret.

From Indian Corps to 51st (Highland), Lahore and Meerut Divisions, No. G.139, dated 6-7-15.

The following signals, in addition to those recently ordered in the case of gas attack, will be used as alarm signals throughout the Indian Corps by night.

(a) "Enemy Infantry Attacking."

Green rocket followed immediately by a white rocket sent up from vicinity of point attacked, and repeated once after a two minute interval.

(b) "Heavy Artillery or Trench Mortar Bombardment of our Trenches."

Green rocket followed immediately by a red rocket sent up and repeated in a similar manner.

Parachute (asteroid) rockets are to be used for this purpose, and for no other. These signals are to be considered as supplementary to and not in substitution of other means of communication such as telephone.

Special alarm signals of this nature for infantry or artillery attacks are not considered necessary by day or for so long as Artillery Observation Officers are at their posts and can see our trenches from them.

19th Division

For information.

(Sd) W. C. Bannatyne, Capt,
General Staff.

Indian Corps.

SECRET  G.A.53.

To:-
    A.A.&.Q.M.G.
    O.C. Divl.Squadron.
    " " Cyclists.
    " " M.M.G.Battery.
    C.R.E.
    Headquarters, Divl.R.A.
    " 56th Infantry Brigade.
    " 57th " "
    " 58th " "
    O.C. 5th South Wales Borderers.
    O.C. Divl.Signal Company.
    " " Train.
    A.D.M.S.

****

    The front line held by the Indian Corps will in future be divided into four sections, each held by a Brigade.

    These sections will be numbered from right to left, Ind 1, Ind 2, Ind 3, Ind 4.

    Each Brigade Section will be subdivided into sub-sections which will be lettered A,B,C,&c. from the right of the section.

    Thus Ind 1 A will indicate the right subsection of the right brigade; Ind 2 B will mean the second subsection of the second brigade from the right of the Corps; and so on.

                                                 A. Buckle

H.Q.19th Divn.   Lieut-Colonel.
17/8/15.   General Staff.

CONFIDENTIAL.

19th Division No. I.201.

TO :-
   ALL UNITS.

      A case has come to notice of persons acting in a very suspicious manner having been allowed to leave a certain area, (where troops were billeted) without any steps having been taken to investigate their movements.

2.   It is, therefore, notified for information that the following are the means of thoroughly investigating any similar cases.

3.   The A.P.M. should at once be notified and he can then employ either British Police or French Gendarmerie - if need be British or French detectives to make a searching enquiry into any suspicious cases.

4.   Should there be any probability of the early departure of the suspected persons, they should be detained pending the A.P.M's enquiry. It is, as a general rule, more desirable to watch than to detain suspected persons, so long as they remain in any defined area, but it is essential to inform the A.P.M. as early as possible.

H.Q.19th Division,
21st August 1915.

                          Major,
                        General Staff.

R

Copy No. 15

19th Division Order No.6.

26th August 1915.

References to (a) 1/40,000 Map,
(b) Tracings of trench map issued to Brigades herewith.

Information.	1.	The Indian Corps is taking up the front from A 9 a 5.9. to WINCHESTER ROAD (H 25 d), both inclusive, by 6 a.m. 1st September; 19th Divn. on the right, on a front of two brigades; Lahore Divn. in the centre, on a front of one brigade; and Meerut Divn. on the left, with two brigades in front line.
Intention.	2.	The 19th Divn. will relieve part of the 2nd Divn. and the 7th Divn. on the portion of the front extending from GRENADIER ROAD Communication trench (A 9 a 5.9.) inclusive, to FARM CORNER (S 15 b 2.2.) ~~exclusive.~~
Distribution.	3.	The front will be divided into two sections, as follows:-
58th Bde.		(a) 58th Brigade will take up the right section, from the right as far as approximately the left end of the subsection at present known as "C 2", including PIONEER ROAD Communication trench. Headquarters right section - LOISNE.
57th Bde.		(b) 57th Brigade will take up the line from the left of "C 2" to the left of the Divisional front. Headquarters left section, CSE. DU RAUX.

Each of these Brigades will have three battalions in front line and one in reserve. Detailed instructions are being issued separately to Infantry Brigades.

The exact line of demarcation on the front line trenches between sections will be adjusted by G.Os.C. Brigades after the occupation of the line.

58th Brigade on its right takes over approximately one subsection from the left Brigade of 2nd Divn., arranging direct with that Brigade, the Headquarters of which are at F 11 c 0.9; the remainder from the right Brigade of 7th Divn.

57th Bde. on its right takes over one subsection from the right Brigade of 7th Divn., the remainder from the left Brigade.

56th Bde.		(c) 56th Brigade will be in Army Reserve in the area LES LOBES --- LAWE CANAL --- LES CHOQUAUX --- LA TOMBE WILLOT, in accordance with separate instructions issued to Staff Captain. Headquarters Reserve Brigade -- W 6 d 4.6.
Brigade Areas.	4.	Brigade Areas are shown on the First Army Area Map issued to Brigades. Responsibility for posts and other defences will coincide with these areas. As regards the Front System these boundaries are shown on a larger scale on the trench map tracings.
Artillery.	5.	Artillery reliefs will be completed by 6 a.m. on 28th August, in accordance with instructions issued to those concerned under this office G.A.67 of 25rd instant.
Moves	6.	Movements in relief will take place in accordance with the attached March Table.

7.

Progress of reliefs.	7.	Daily progress of reliefs will be reported to Divisional Head Quarters.
Refilling Points.	8.	Separate instructions as to the arrangements to be made for refilling have been issued to all concerned.
Reports.	9.	To HERVILLE up to 10-0 a.m. 31st August, then to LOCON.

Issued at 5-0 p.m.

A.S.Buckle

Lieut-Colonel,

General Staff.

Copy No.	To whom issued.
1.	File.
2) 3)	War Diary.
4.	G.O.C.
5.	G.S.
6.	A.A.G.Q.M.G.
7-9.	G.O.C., R.A.
10.	C.R.E.
11.	56th Infy. Bde.
12.	57th " "
13.	58th " "
14.	Divnl. Cavalry.
15.	Divnl. Cyclists.
16.	M.M.G.Battery.
17.	5/S.W.Borderers (Pioneers).
18.	Divnl. Train.
19.	A.D.M.S.
20.- 21.	Indian Corps.
22.	Lahore Division.
23.	Meerut Division.
24.	Divnl. Signal Coy.
25.	1st Corps.
26.	2nd Division.
27.	7th Division.

S E C R E T.

G.A.60

Headquarters,
    57th Infantry Brigade.
    58th   "   "

    Now that the line has been taken over by the Division the Major-General Commanding desires you to direct your particular attention to the work to be done. There is so much to be done, both in improving the defensive power of the line with the least possible delay, and in preparing for its occupation in the winter, that the work must be pressed forward with the utmost energy. In carrying it out it is to be distinctly understood that the principles of design and construction decided upon at the recent Divisional Conference, and issued in the Memorandum G.A.60 of 23rd August, are to be closely followed.

2.   The organisation for work will at present be as laid down in the attached memorandum; the chief object now being to improve the defences for tactical use under the present summer conditions, while the preparations for the winter are for a short time to be a subordinate matter.

3.   You will assemble your Commanding Officers as soon as practicable with a view to ensuring that as much work as possible is carried out daily by those under their command in the subsections for which they are responsible. Men on sentry or patrol duty must be given the necessary rest, but every other available man is to be employed to the full extent of his powers. Certain portions of the work can only be done at night, but there is much that can be done by day; constant personal supervision by officers is essential to see that no time is wasted. The matter is urgent, and great efforts will be required from all ranks, not only on the present improvement of

the

the defences but continuously until the preparations for the winter are complete.

H.Q.19th Divn
31/8/15.

Lieut-Colonel.
General Staff.

Copies for information to:-

       56th Infantry Brigade.
       5th South Wales Borderers.
       C.R.E.
       O.C.Divl.Squadron.
       O.C.Cyclist Company.

Secret.   G.A.52.

O.C. Divisional Cavalry.
  ,,   ,,   Cyclists.
Headquarters 57th Brigade.

The attached extract from the Divisional Defence Scheme, which is now being compiled, is forwarded for information and guidance. The completed Defence Scheme will give the permanent defensive measures taken to meet a local hostile attack on the Divisional front only, and has no concern with other operations.

H.Q. 19th Division,   Lieutenant-Colonel,
14th September 1915.   General Staff.

* * * * *

Secret

ACTION OF TROOPS IN RESERVE.

[Stamp: 15 SEP.1915 ...DIV. CYCLIST CO.]

1. The Brigade in Reserve is not normally available for use in support of the Brigades in front line, as it is in Army Reserve. In the event, however, of a local hostile attack on the front held by the 19th Division, it is probable that permission for its temporary employment by the Divisional Commander will be obtained.

    In this event:-

    (a) Should the enemy penetrate the defences in IND I, the Brigade in reserve about LOCON will assemble W of GORRE, forming up about F 3 a and b.

    Routes. Battalions N of LOCON cross roads, and Brigade H.Q. -- by LOCON cross roads -- PONT TOURNANT -- MESPLAUX -- X 21 central -- road junction X 27 c.

    Battalions S of LOCON cross roads -- by trestle bridge at X 13 d 7.9., along canal bank to X 13 d 4.1. -- X 20 c 5.3 -- track (not marked on map) through X 26 a and c to LA CROIX DE FER -- F 2 b 4.1.

    (b) Should the enemy penetrate the defences in IND II, the Brigade in reserve will assemble W of LE TOURET, X 16 a and c.

    Routes. Battalions N of LOCON cross roads -- by road junction X 1 d 7.9. -- trestle bridge at X 8 b 1.1. -- X 8 b 4.4. -- X 15 b 2.8.

    Battalions S of LOCON cross roads and Brigade H.Q.- by LOCON cross roads -- PONT TOURNANT -- MESPLAUX-- LES FACONS -- X 21 a 9.9.

    Each Brigade going into Reserve for the first time will send out officers to reconnoitre the above routes and forming-up places as soon as possible after it goes into Reserve.

2. The Divisional Cavalry and Cyclists will assemble at their alarm posts, sending 4 orderlies each to Divisional Headquarters.

* * * * *

H.Q.19th Division,
14th September 1915.

Lieutenant-Colonel,
General Staff.

CONFIDENTIAL.   No.774/1 (A).

H.Q., Lahore Division.
H.Q., Meerut Division.
H.Q., 19th Division.

   Should any case occur of a British Officer or Soldier being served with a summons to appear before a French Court, it is to be reported to this office and the officer or soldier is not to be allowed to appear in the Court until further instructions are received by you.

   To enable these instructions to be issued before date on which the officer or soldier is required to attend the Court, please issue such orders as you may consider necessary to ensure the prompt reporting of such cases

   No reference should be made to this subject in Routine Orders.

                                          A. Dickson. Major,
                                          D.A.A. & Q.M.G., Indian Corps.

H.Q., Indian Corps,
   14/9/15.

Copy forwarded for information and necessary action
to:-

_____

                                          A. Dickson. Major,
                                          D.A.A. & Q.M.G., Indian Corps.

P.T.O.

19th Division No. A/1065/L.

To All Units.

For information and guidance. In every case when a British Officer or Soldier is summoned to appear before a French Court a telegram is to be sent through the usual channels to Divisional H.Q., reporting the case and asking for instructions. A written report of the facts of the case should follow without any delay.

In no circumstances will a British Officer or soldier appear before a French Court without specific instructions from this office.

M Davies

D H.Q.,
15/9/15.

Lieut-Colonel,
A.A. & Q.M.G., 19th Division.

Divl. Cyclists

Copy No 15

19th Division Order No 7
****

12th September 1915.

References to 1/40,000 Combined Sheet, BETHUNE.

1. 56th Brigade will relieve 57th Brigade in IND II on night of 13th/14th inst. Garrisons of posts and keeps may be relieved on the afternoon of 13th; no other movement E of RUE DE L'EPINETTE before 7-30 p.m. Details of relief will be arranged between Brigades concerned.

2. There will be no change in Artillery or Engineer dispositions.

3. 57th Brigade will report to Divl.H.Q. when the relief is complete.

4. Brigadier-General B.G.Lewis, D.S.O. will assume command of IND II from 10 a.m. on 14th instant.

Issued at 4-15 p.m.

Lieut-Colonel.
General Staff.

To whom issued

File
War Diary.
G.O.C.
G.S.
A.A.&.Q.M.G.
G.O.C.,R.A.
C.R.E.
56th Infantry Brigade.
57th   ,,   ,,
58th   ,,   ,,
Divl.Cavalry.
Divl.Cyclists.
5th South Wales Borderers (Pnrs)
Divl.Train.
A.D.M.S.
Indian Corps.
Lahore Division.
Meerut Division.
Divl.Signal Coy.
2nd Division.

Correction Slip - O.O. No. 65 of 19-9-15.

(i) In line 11 of para:5 (a) for "58th Bde" read "56th Bde".

(ii) Para. 6 is cancelled. Further orders will issue re Advanced Report Centres. Reports to present H.Q.

H.Q.19th Division,
19th September 1915.

Major, G.S.,
19th Division.

Copy No 15

19th Division Order No 8.

19th September 1915.

References to 1/40,000 Combined Sheet, BETHUNE,
and to Corps Trench Map.

Information.	1	Information has already been issued to those directly concerned under G.A.80 of 15th inst.
Intention.	2.	The Division will be redistributed in view of forthcoming operations.
Distribution. 56th Brigade.	3. (a)	56th Bde. will extend the front now occupied by it to the right as far as BARNTON ROAD exclusive. The additional portion of front will be taken over from 58th Bde., under arrangements to be made between Brigadiers, on the night of 20th/21st inst. The CAILLOUX posts (S 25 b 8.7.) will be taken over by 56th Bde., but FESTUBERT and FESTUBERT EAST will remain in IND I. The machine guns of 5th S.W.B. will come under the orders of G.O.C. 56th Bde for employment as reserve machine guns in IND II.
58th Brigade.	(b)	On the relief of the left battalion of 58th Bde. by a battalion of 56th Bde. as above, a battalion of 58th Bde. will go into Brigade Reserve in the vicinity of the Northern portion of the "Intermediate Line".
5th S.W.B.	(c)	The machine gun section of 5th S.W.B. will be sent to H.Q. 56th Bde. at CSE. DU RAUX on 20th inst., time to be arranged by G.O.C. 56th Bde.
Divisional Artillery.	(d)	The Divisional Artillery will remain grouped as at present for the preliminary operations.
Medical.	4.	Advanced Dressing Stations. F 5 central. X 11 b 3.3. Main Dressing Stations. MESPLAUX .... X 14 a 10.7. BOIS DE PACAUT ..... Q 33 b 6.6. EGLISE .... Q 24 c 6.8.
Ammunition and Supplies	5.	Supply of ammunition and refilling of supplies as at present.
Reports.	6.	Advanced Report Centres will be occupied from 8 p.m. 20th inst., as follows:- Divisional ....LOISNE, X 28 a 8.8. 56th Bde..............RUE DE CAILLOUX, S 20 c 6.2. 58th Bde.............."WELSH CHAPEL", LE PLANTIN, A 1 d 6.9.

A.C.Butler
Lieutenant-Colonel.
General Staff.

Issued at 2-30 p.m.

Copies to:-

File	Divl.Cavalry.
War Diary	Divl.Cyclists.
G.O.C.	5th S.Wales Borderers.
G.S.	Divl.Train.
A.A.&.Q.M.G.	A.D.M.S.
G.O.C.,R.A.	Indian Corps.
C.R.E.	Lahore Division.
56th Infantry Brigade.	Meerut Division.
57th ,, ,,	Divl.Signal Coy.
58th ,, ,,	2nd Division.

Dinl Cyclists Co

Secret.

With reference to 19th Division Order No. 10 of 28th instant, para. 3 (b), PIONEER ROAD will be included in IND II, and not IND III as stated. CAILLOUX posts will also eventually be included in IND II, but orders for the relief of 56th Bde. in these posts by 57th Bde. will be issued later.

A.S.... (signature)
Lieutenant-Colonel, G.S.,
19th Division.

Advd.H.Q.19th Division,
29th September 1915.

(Issued to all recipients of Division Order No.10 except Lahore, Meerut and 2nd Divisions).

leychsb (handwritten)

19th Division Order No. 10.   Copy No. 16

28th September 1915.

References to 1/40,000 Combined Sheet BETHUNE,
and Corps Trench Map.

Information   1.   The Indian Corps is handing over to 3rd Corps a portion of its front on the North. On the South it will take over the front held by the 5th Bde. of 2nd Divn., from the present right of 19th Divn. as far as the LA BASSEE Canal.

The Sirhind Bde. of Lahore Divn., with the 1st Bn. Seaforth Highlanders from Meerut Divn., is on its way to GORRE. On arrival there it is to come under the orders of G.O.C. 19th Divn.

No. 176 (Tunnelling) Coy. R.E. remains at GORRE for duty in the GIVENCHY Section as at present.

Infantry moves   2.   (a). Sirhind Bde. plus 1st Seaforths will take over
on 28th Sept.   this evening the front now held by 5th Bde. of 2nd Divn., from the right of 19th Divn. (A 3 c 3.0.) to the LA BASSEE Canal. Under instructions from Indian Corps the two sub-sections on the GIVENCHY ridge will be held by the 1st H.L.I. and 1st Seaforths. Arrangements to be made direct by G.O.C. Sirhind Bde. with G.O.C. 5th Bde. This Section will, from 8 p.m. to-day, be known as IND I.

                       (b). The garrisons or guards furnished by 5/S.W.B. on defended localities and posts in the present IND I will be relieved this evening by 58th Bde., which will also furnish, as before, the caretaking guards withdrawn from certain posts under 19th Division Order No.9 of 22nd inst., para.4 (b).

Reliefs, night   3.   On the night of 29th/30th inst :-
of 29/30 Sept.   (a). 57th Bde. will relieve 58th Bde. on its present front with two battalions, and will take over the present right subsection held by 56th Bde. with a third battalion (left of the 57th Bde. front at S 27 b 4.3½); the fourth battalion of 57th Bde. will be in Divisional Reserve in the "Intermediate Line". This section will, from 8 p.m. today, be known as IND II.

                       (b). 56th Bde., on the relief of its right battalion by a battalion of 57th Bde., as above, will hold the CANADIAN ORCHARD Salient, from S 27 b 4.3½ to QUINQUE CROSSING, with one battalion, and the remainder of its front with two battalions, as originally subdivided. The battalion of 56th Bde. in Divnl. Reserve will remain in its present position.
CAILLOUX posts and PIONEER ROAD will remain in this Section, which, from 8 p.m. today, will be known as IND III.
On 30th inst. the machine-guns of 5/S.W.B. at present under G.O.C.56th Bde., will return to their battalion.

                       (c). 58th Bde., on relief, will be in Army Reserve, in the billeting area about LE HAMEL now occupied by 57th Bde.

Command of Sections.	4.	Command of Sections of the line will be taken over by relieving brigadiers on completion of reliefs.
Artillery.	5.	No Artillery reliefs will take place for the present. The Artillery of 2nd Divn., on North of Canal, now covering the front to be taken over from 2nd Divn., will continue to cover that front, and will be under the command of G.O.C. R.A. 19th Division.
Engineers.	6.	The 81st Field Co.R.E. will move to GORRE to-morrow, 29th, and take over the R.E. duties in the new IND I under arrangements to be made by C.R.E. One section will be at disposal of G.O.C. Sirhind Bde., and the O.C. 81st Field Co. will act as his R.E. adviser.
Billeting Areas.	7.	Billeting areas of the new IND II and III will remain as at present; of the new IND I will be notified as soon as settled by D.A. & Q.M.G. Indian Corps.
Supply.	8.	Supply arrangements for Sirhind Bde. and 1/Seaforths will be made by Lahore Divn.; for troops of 19th Divn. as at present.
Progress of Reliefs.	9.	Progress of reliefs will be reported.
Reports.	10.	Sirhind Bde. Report Centre...F 10 d 8.9.
58th Bde. ,, ,, ...A 1 d 6.9.
56th Bde. ,, ,, ...S 20 c 5.2.
57th Bde. ,, ,, ...X 20 b 7.1.
19th Divn. ,, ,, ...X 23 a 8.8.

Lieutenant-Colonel, G.S.
19th Division.

Issued at 6-30 p.m.

Copies to :-

File.
War Diary.
G.O.C.
G.S.
A.A.& Q.M.G.
G.O.C.,R.A.
C.R.E.
56th Infantry Brigade.
57th ,, ,,
58th ,, ,,
Divnl.Cavalry.
,, Cyclists.

5th S.Wales Borderers.
Divnl. Train.
M.M.G.Battery.
A.R.M.S.
Indian Corps.
Lahore Division.
Meerut Division.
Divnl. Signal Coy.
2nd Division.
Sirhind Brigade.

121/7/53

19th Division

19th Divl: Cyclist Coy.
Vol 2
Sep / 15

in fighting vicinity
of Bethune.
3/11/15

Army Form C. 2118

WAR DIARY
or
INTELLIGENCE SUMMARY
(Erase heading not required.)

Confidential
War Diary
of
19. Divisional Signal Company
From: 20/9/15
to 26/11/15
Volume II.

Army Form C. 2118

WAR DIARY or INTELLIGENCE SUMMARY

(Erase heading not required.)

Sheet No. 6.

Place	Date	Hour	Summary of Events and Information	Remarks and references to Appendices
HINGETTE	20/9/15		Weather fine, clear and dry. Hazy early morning. Received memorandum entitled "Instructions for Collection and Disposal of Prisoners of War" dated 1/9/15 from D.H.Q. It is notified in this memorandum that K. 19th Division Collecting Station will be established in L.E. Point X.16.d.4.8 on the contour of BETHUNE. Co.s. collecting station at FOSSE. D.H.S. near that Lt. ST. MOILLIET remain with Salange Co. until further order.	
	21/9/15		Weather on 20/9/15. 28 NCOs, men were detailed to form permanent D.H.B. guard. This Guard Relieved for 24 hrs. proceeded to D.H.B. under 2/Lt. R. TALBOT and reported to Camp Commandant there at 9 a.m. 50 NCOs, men (Infantry) detailed by the Adjt for return were inclined — return instead to come on returns by this Unit for rations were inclined — return instead to Salvage Co. Wagon to the until there by Lt. ST.MOILLIET and 4 NCOs, men of this Company till remaining with Salvage Co. *Army Corps. R.O. No. 136. Caution against enteric fever. Repeated Company order. The following is an extract from Company Orders:- "This Company has now been supplied with a Lyger Stone and arrangements are being made to write to the Works every night. Then before coming on parade will see that their water bottles are filled from this source. A Special order issued daily will distribution etc. of the Company in the event of a sudden move, see Appendix. No. 6430. L/Cpl Sherriss evacuated sick to Casualty Clearing Station LILLERS.	See Appendix I.
	22/9/15		Weather fine and so on 21/9/15. No. 6472. Pte Merryfield P was on 21/9/15 evacuated sick out of Divisional area to No. 6. Casualty Clearing Hospital. No. 5088 L/Cpl Dodd L has been evacuated but no official information has been received by this unit. (Note: Medical services must report when men are admitted or discharged tempy. anything outside mentioning Hospital, so when men are sent — until out of Division.)	

WAR DIARY or INTELLIGENCE SUMMARY

Army Form C. 2118

Sheet No. 7

Place	Date	Hour	Summary of Events and Information	Remarks and references to Appendices
HINGETTE	23/9/15		Weather fine & dry until evening. Wind from heavy. Two tents went round 5 PM. Sunk. Heavy rain with thunder and much lightning at 7.30 PM. Received instructions and instructions re forthcoming operation. See appendix. 40 NCOs and men were detailed for duties in Troops Control PO6 and Stragglers PO6, under A.P.M. 19 D.H.Q.	See Appendix I
	24/9/15		Weather: Dull & misty. Word from E. n S.E. Received DHO instructions and instructions re forthcoming operations. 6 NCOs were added to existing H.Q. Guard. 28 Reserves. For duties with D.H.Q. where Divisional advanced Refm Centre opened.	See Appendix II
	25/9/15		Weather: wet, dull & misty. Wind from E.n S.E. Received orders from H.Q., Divisional Squadron to send 2 Officers and NCOs and men to right of H. APM. L. X. 16. d. 39. (Combined Chief BETHUNE) & act no escort/dispersal. Received orders from H. 19 Divisional Squadron to remain in present billets and await instructions & bright letter to K. 154 Coy A.S.C. stating D.H.Q. had to yet orders for this unit to return supply wagon & must move to his area as 17 D.19 Divisional train to commanded M.46 form H. 19 D.T. when R.T.H.Q. CO. wrote letter to D.H.Q. & pointing authority to supply wagon to return to this unit.	See Appendix I
	26/9/15		Weather: fine, very clear. Wind from E n S.E. Horses examined by Veterinary Officer. Received orders from Corps AD Vet. Inspection to make sure Squadron & make sure our Battalion defects & two units were inspect immediately collectively stated in new and kept & suitable accommoda.	See Appendix II

Army Form C. 2118

WAR DIARY
or
INTELLIGENCE SUMMARY
(Erase heading not required.)

Appendix II

Place	Date	Hour	Summary of Events and Information	Remarks and references to Appendices
			Summary of Information and Orders received in forwarding battle Summarised by J.C.S. WHITTUCK, Lieut, 19. Division Cyclist Co. 27/9/15.	

Orders Received
1. G.A. 30/5 dated 21/9/15 from 19. D.H.Q. - Revised instructions re accessory. Rec'd 23/9/15
2. 19. Div'l Order. No. 9. Copy No. 11, dated 22/9/15 from D.H.Q. - Received 23/9/15
3. G.A. 30/8 dated 22/9/15 from 19. D.H.Q. - 19. Division Instructions - Received 23/9/15
4. A/65/2 dated 21/9/15 - Instructions re Clearing Battlefield, handed personally to C.O. of D.H.Q. on 23/9/15.
5. 19. Div'l Artillery Arrangements (no date) - Received 23/9/15.
6. Additions and Amendments to Div'l Order. No. 9. Copy No. 15 dated 24/9/15 from D.H.Q. - Received 24/9/15.

Extract from 19. Div'l Order No. 9, dated 22/9/15.
"Mounted Corps II: "The Div'l Squadron and Div'l Cyclist Co. will be employed detailed for duties in connection with control posts, bridge guards, salvage and prisoners, vide separate instructions issued herewith. They will however be prepared to move forward when called upon to tactical employment at a later stage.
" In the event of a general advance. The Div'l Squadron will furnish
" 1 NCO and 3 men and the Div'l Cyclist Co. 4 NCO's + 30 men in party with D.H.Q. when the Advanced Divisional Report Centre is formed. The Present D.H.Q.
" Guard at LICON will form part of this party."

Extract from "Instructions re Clearing of Battlefield" 19. Division, A/65/2 dated 21/9/15.
"Para 3. B.C.D. General arrangements. The Div'l Squadron + Div'l Cyclists, assisted by the Salvage Co. will perform all duties in connection with (1) Disposal of prisoners (2) Burial of the dead (3) Collection and disposal of war material, until the

WAR DIARY or INTELLIGENCE SUMMARY

Army Form C. 2118

Appendix II Sheet 2.

"are required for the advance to duty as mounted troops"

| Duty | Troops available | Refords 6 | at Whatfleurs | Sub. |

Clearing Battlefield — 2 in/Graham (less 2 Troops) 2 in/Cyclists (1st Platoon) i/charge O.C.

Prisoners Escort to LOCON — A.P.M. — LE TOURET

Prisoners Guard and Escort at LOCON — 2 Troops 2in/ Graham — Bn 3/n Ingham D.H.Q. — LOCON

"4. B. Schools instructions have been issued regarding the collection & disposal of prisoners of war."

"5. C. Burial of the dead. If circumstances permit the dead will be collected and taken from the battlefield by teams to which 6 cemeteries at LE TOURET – FESTUBERT – BROWNS ROAD – RUE DES BERCEAUX. Bodies will be taken from Fd Ambulances & LOCAN Cemetery where circumstances do not permit of bodies being taken to the cemeteries evenly the burymust take place will be selected on burial places."

"6. D. Collection & disposal of all war material, equipment, supplies etc. The escorting charge of Co.P. will be the method of the collecting party assisted by 2in/ Graham & Bin 1. "Cyclists and further expanded by civil labour if to found necessary.

WAR DIARY or INTELLIGENCE SUMMARY

Appendix II Sheet 3.

"8. The whole under the Command of Major Ingham (INGHAM), Divi'l Gradner."

"9. The men & the cleanup is divided into two sections corresponding to the "fronts" now held by Brigades: IND.I section — IND.II section."

"10. Trucks detailed for the work: Divisional Gradner. (YORKSHIRE DRAGOONS) —
Divisional Salvage Corps.
Allotment of men, etc.

1 Officer and 30 men Div'l Gradner
40 " Div'l Salvage
NCO " 15 " Salvage Corps. } IND I.

1 Officer and 30 men Div'l Gradner
1 " " 40 " Div'l Cyclists
" " 15 " Salvage Co.
1 NCO } IND II.

"11. A detailed list of local transport available for him is attached. Cars are allotted as follows:
A } IND I. 10 & 15 cwt
B }
C } IND II. 10 & 15 cwt
D } require these cars as required."

"Major Ingham will arrange & requisition these cars as required."

Message from O.C. 19.Div'l Gdnr C. & O.C. 19. Div'l Gradner. and vice versa.

1. A.168 dated 23/9/15 from O.C. H.S.C.C. & O.C. G. Gnd, "On receipt of Telegram & more before advance H.Q. two Co's of Point S.7.E.8.8 (BETHUNE. Confirmed that) near This by H.Q. & work clearing battlefield for Divn. IND I. am kindly reply whether these arrangement satisfactory for you —

2. Form O.C. G. Gnd., numbered & dated, F.K.M.D.C.C., rec'd 23/9/15 — H.Q. M Clearing "battlefield at point S.7.E.8.8. quite satisfactory. I am sure shall have I think " from available men & more equally between IND I and IND II as the N.Reps are " available. This improves by the 3 this afternoon so we can arrange " held for work over here this morning and I can communicate particulars received yesterday;
" method of doing work and "

Army Form C. 2118

WAR DIARY
or
INTELLIGENCE SUMMARY
(Erase heading not required.)

Appendix II Sheet 4.

Place	Date	Hour	Summary of Events and Information	Remarks and references to Appendices

3. A.71 dated 23/9/15 from O.C. F.A. D.Sqnd. "Your message received now will be with you this morning between 11 & 12. Select an escort that have very fit men available, and for work clearing battlefield, as fifteen N.C.O.s & men are taken away for duty on 19. Div Order No.7. Sec.11 requiring
" " the N.C.O. & 30 men for duty with D.H.Q. When advanced rejnt centre is formed
" " any N.C.O. can be taken. I am not apt with about 50 N.C.O.s available for
" " any front clearing battlefield."

4. A.176 dated 24/9/15 from O.C. F.C.E. 5 O.C. D.Sqnd. "Have received no information of
" " a plan re clearing battlefield nor is it intended for me to make one. I
" " am copy now & to will send officer early super & tracing and
" " have for the staffs attached in our H.Q. Division the letter to this months
" " my H.Q. for this and I will ask all messages have through you."

5. From O.C. 19 Div Sqnd, unnumbered & undated, to O.C. D.C.C. "I am just starting
" " a O.gr. & H.Q. & will enquire about sun plans & copy & instructions say
" " & will also mention other points sun raise and rank you message later
" " in the day."   Rec'd 27/9/15

6. From O.C. 19.D. Sqnd, unnumbered & undated, O.C. D.C.C. "No orders for you from C
" " do at present in connection clearing battlefield and remain at your
" " present billets pending further instructions."

7. From O.C. 19.D. Sqnd, unnumbered & undated, O.M. D.C.C. rec'd 26/9/15
" " Instructions received please make yourself acquainted with Brig locality of
" " Battalion Aid & dressing stations, and report of suitable Collecting Stations
" " between these and nearest 2 intermediate evacuation available and if necessary
" " arrange with owner for use of same.

Army Form C. 2118

WAR DIARY
or
INTELLIGENCE SUMMARY

(Erase heading not required.) Appendix II. Sheet 5.

Place	Date	Hour	Summary of Events and Information	Remarks and references to Appendices
			8. O.4 dated 26/9/15 from H. D.C.C. & H.D. Agent. "Reference our minute as all arrangements made with 5T. Brigade & their liaison" "In towing material behind mechanical or horse transport" "Collecting claims not necessary and recommendation regards no" "shall require several carts for hauling material from the ends of the" "Tramlines 5 Septr."	

Army Form C. 2118

WAR DIARY
or
INTELLIGENCE SUMMARY
(Erase heading not required.)

Sheet No. 8.

Place	Date	Hour	Summary of Events and Information	Remarks and references to Appendices
HINGETTE	27/9/15		Weather, wet & dull - O/r dated 27/9/15 from H.Q. 19 D.C.C. [Camp Commandant 19 Div]. arrangements war of Divisional Letter at LOCON for Division 28/9/15	J.C.W.
	28/9/15		Weather damp and cold. O/r dated 28/9/15 from H.Q. 19 D.C.C. L A.P.M. 19 Division notifying him that men of the Company will from tomorrow wear brassards instead of whistle	J.C.W.
	29/9/15		Weather dull with continuous rain. Boys sent to Corps Cart evacuated sick from 3rd British Field Ambulance. Received O/r of Divisional order No. 10. City No. 16 dated 29/9/15 notifying that the Indian Corps is taking over a portion of the front on the north. One section it will take over the front held by 5 & 8 Bde & 2nd Division, from the present right of 19 Div. as far as the LA BASSÉE Canal, also notifying notice of the various unit concerned	J.C.W.
	30/9/15		Weather dry, bright & clear. Strong wind from N.W. No. 4334 Private Warburton R evacuated sick out of Dist. and Divisional enquiries and list where allowance for officers also commented ing. Clined field allowance from 27/4/15 to R.E. Company Lieutenant Major N. O/18 dated 30/9/15 from R.E. 19 D.C.C. to R.E. 19 Div Salvage Co. stating that no 19.D.C.C. future supplies will the forwarded by C.T. Ebert. O/19 dated 30/9/15 from H.Q. 19 D.C.C. Re referred brigade front they may now be followed by transport the new and-cold. Birds from N.W.	J.C.W.
	1/10/15		Weather. O/19 dated 30/9/15 from H.Q. 19 D.C.C. L A.P.M. 19 Div. "to have any important papers of the brigade O/o dated 30/9/15 from the A. and Command in an the prisoners about lately returned to "Troops it humbled the Doughboys has unable to climb otherwise and climb the not the cave until "have any injection of the end of this week to my relieving there with other men from the muster T.C.	J.C.W.
	2/10/15		Weather fine & dry. Word from M.W. Cdt. A/43 dated 2/10/15 from D.H.Q. "Reconnaitre "PACAUT for Billets & later meet and report result. Lieutenant also going there. "O.C. D.C.C. O/25 dated 2/10/15 "there is continued billets at PACAUT and some there in this "unit but not for both. An understood injunction have made arrangements to billet Clay	J.C.W.
	3/10/15		Weather fine & dry. Cdt. Report into Hills of PACAUT about front Q.25.C.3.7 (not BETHUNE control Billet).	J.C.W.

19th Division Cyclist Company.

APPENDIX I

In the event of this Company being ordered to move suddenly the following instructions are to be followed,

The whole Company will parade with the exception of the following:-

(a) Officers servants.
(b) Corporal Chard & two men of the Sanitary Party
(c) Two cooks & the butcher
(d) The Artificers.
(e) Quarter Master Sergeant Hill & Corporal Draper.
(f) Pte Greedy
(g) The First Line Transport.
(h) The Second Line Transport.
(i) Any man under the doctor & unfit to move
(k) Lnce Cpl. Layzell.
(l) Lnce Cpl. Garbett, Pte Gruning & Pte Purcell

The whole of this party will be under Lt. Whittuck while they are in camp. They will be dealt with as under:-

(a) The Officers servants will pack their masters kits & load them on the baggage wagon and then come out as a party (with the exception of Pte Potter) to find H.Q of the Company.

(b) Corporal Chard will fill in all latrines and tidy up the camp & remain under Lieut. J.B.S. Whittuck until such time as he may decide. These men will be available under Lieut. Whittuck for messengers & to ascertain where the Company has gone.

(c) The two cooks & the butcher will clean, & pack up all camp kettles etc. & attach themselves to the Quarter Master Sergeant.

(d) The Artificers will pack up all their equiptment & load all spare bicycles on the baggage wagon & proceed with the Officers servants to report to the Company H.Q.

(e) Quarter Master Sergt Hill will remain in the camp to pack up the baggage wagon. Corporal Draper will proceed to the 154th Coy A.S.C. of the 19th Divisional Train to procure supply wagon & return with it to camp. As soon as the wagon is packed with all available stores at the moment. Camp kettles, butchers tools & Officers mess kit, both wagons supply & baggage will return to 154th Coy A.S.C. 19th Divisional Train with the Quarter Master Sergt, company cooks & butcher.

(f) Pte Creedy will procure the O.C's Motor cycle or ordinary cycle & put himself at the disposal of Lieut. Whittuck for keeping in touch with the Company H.Q.

(g) As soon as the camp is hurriedly cleared the orderly papers packed up, & boxes packed & loaded on the baggage wagon Lieut Whittuck will proceed to the

Company with the first line transport. He will send on to report the position of the first line transport from time to time so that this can be brought up for further supply of ammunition whenever it is required

(J) Any man unfit to cycle will be brought on the transport wagon if possible, otherwise they will be left, & their position reported to the nearest Unit not moving at the time. Lieut. Whittuck will arrange for this to be done. Their cycles should be brought on in the transport if possible.

(K) Lnce Cpl. Layzell will as soon as possible pack up all orderly papers etc, & make arrangements to convey them to the baggage wagon. He will then be under Lieut. Whittuck for further orders

(L) Lnce Cpl. Garbett, Pte Greening & Pte Purcell will pack up the officers mess kit & load it on the baggage wagon, & then cycle out with the officers servants & artificers, to report to Company H. Q.

Lnce Cpl. Garbett will be in charge of this party. They will be informed of the route Company H. Q's. has gone by Pte Creedy. Pte Bainbridge immediately rejoins his platoon.

50 Rounds of ammunition will be issued to every man as soon as they fall in on the parade ground also one blanket per man.

This will be done by the Company Sgt. Major. H. Q signalers & H.Q's not mentioned above will move with the C. O. & unless otherwise ordered will remain close to him.

Orders by
A Herbert Smith
Capt.
O.C. 19th Divisional Cyclist Coy

21.9.15.

SECRET.   G.A.80/5.

REVISED INSTRUCTIONS RE ACCESSORY.

The instructions with reference to accessory given in this office G.A.80/2 of 15-9-15 are cancelled, and the following substituted, the time of the beginning of the gas attack being reckoned as Zero. It will probably be 4.50 a.m. on 25th instant, but it is expected that the exact hour will be notified about 10 p.m. on 24th.

<u>These instructions only apply if the weather conditions on the morning of the assault admit of the use of accessory;</u> but all necessary preparations must be made beforehand for carrying them out.

1. The whole front of the Indian Corps will be covered by smoke. This smoke will be started everywhere at 0.6 minutes; and will be kept up, except on the actual fronts of the infantry attacks, until 0.40 minutes.

2. The time-table for the gas attack by the 2nd Division on our right (also by the Meerut Division in the Indian Corps) is as follows :-

   0.   - 0.6 Gas, 3 cylinders.
   0.6. - 0.10 Smoke, 2 candles.   At 0.8 they prepare to
                                     assault, using extra
                                     candles from 0.8 to 0.10
                                     to make smoke as dense
                                     as possible.

   0.10 ----- Assault.

3. The above applies also to the gas attack, but does <u>not</u> apply to the smoke attack, in the portion of our front in which gas is installed, viz, from our right to the South end of THE LOOP, which will be carried out by 2nd Division. The men of the 2nd Division who work the smoke in this portion of our front will continue the smoke and stop it in exactly the same way as 58th Bde., see para. 6 below.

4. It should be explained to the troops that the smoke from smoke-candles is quite harmless. As regards phosphorus grenades, while not actually deadly, it is undesirable that troops should attack through the smoke from them, and if they do so the men and their clothing are liable to be burnt by the burning fragments of phosphorus. For these reasons smoke-candles only will be used along the front of 58th Bde. From the right of 56th Bde. as far as the North end of the advanced front trench at ROTHESAY BAY (S 27 c 6.7.) both smoke-candles and phosphorus grenades will be provided; and 2 Gamage catapults will be fixed on the right of 56th Bde. and 2 at the North end of the above mentioned advanced front trench.

If the wind at the time of the assault is West or South of West, the phosphorus grenades will be used all along the 56th Bde. front, and the catapults on the right will be employed to make a barrage of smoke immediately on the left of the advance of 58th Brigade. If, however, the wind is at all North of West, the smoke candles will be used as far North as S 27 c 6.7., and the catapults there will be employed for the barrage. In any case phosphorus grenades will be used along the rest of the front of 56th Bde. to the left.

5.

5.   1050 single and 377 triple smoke-candles are available for the Division; of these the triple candles and 700 single candles are allotted to 58th Bde., and the remaining 350 single candles to 56th Bde. 58th Bde. will hand over the latter at once.

6.   G.O.C. 58th Bde. will be in close touch with the Commander of the Brigade of 2nd Division attacking on his right, and will use his own initiative in stopping the smoke on his Brigade front and starting his Brigade forward to the assault if it is found that the enemy shows any signs of weakening, or when the progress of the attack by 2nd Division renders it possible for 58th Bde. to advance in co-operation.
    Along the rest of the Divisional front the emission of smoke will continue from 0.6 to 0.40, as in 1 above.

7.   In the attacks by 2nd and Meerut Divisions, from 0. to 0.10 the front system of the hostile trenches will be kept under continuous shrapnel fire; defences further in rear under bombardment of H.E. shell of all calibres. At 0.10, when the assault begins the fire of the Artillery covering these Divisions will be lifted as required.
    In the case of the advance of 58th Bde., however, the shrapnel fire on the front trenches will be lifted gradually after 0.10 on to support trenches, and also turned off the Southern end of the RUE D'OUVERT to clear the flank of the advance of 2nd Division; with the exception of one battery which can continue to fire safely on the enemy's front trenches in A 3 a until stopped by the signal for the advance of 58th Bde.
    G.O.C. 58th Bde. will give this signal, which will consist of a sheaf of rockets fired from the Bde. Report Centre.

8. A smoke barrage will be formed by 2nd Divn., with 2" and Stokes mortars, on the left flank of its attack, but clear of the right flank of attack by 58th Bde.

H.Q. 19th Division,
21st September 1915.

Lieut-Colonel,
General Staff,
19th Division.

SECRET.   G.A.30/8.

19th Division - Instructions.

The following General Instructions are issued in connection with forthcoming operations:-

(1) ~~ADVANCED REPORT CENTRES.~~
    ~~The date of establishment of Advanced Divisional and Brigade Report Centres will be notified later.~~

           Divisional Report Centre -- LOISNE, X 28 a 8.8.
           58th Bde.   ,,   ,, -- WELSH CHAPEL A 1 d 5.2.
           ~~56th Bde.   ,,   ,, -- RUE DE CAILLOUX 5 20 c 5.2.~~

    The following will be at the Advanced Divisional Report Centre:-
                    G.O.C.
                    2 A.D.Cs.
                    3 G.S.Os.
                    A.A.&.Q.M.G.
                    H.Q.Divl R.A.
                       ,,   ,, R.E.
    All messages dealing with operations or otherwise concerning the General Staff, and all urgent messages on Administrative subjects will be addressed "Advd.19th Divn."
    All routine messages will be addressed "19th Divn."
    It is essential that messages and letters should be correctly addressed as above.

(2) FORMING UP FOR ASSAULT.
    Every precaution must be taken that, when troops are forming up for the assault, bayonets are not allowed to show over the parapet.

(3) DOCUMENTS.
    Regimental officers are not to carry on their person any documents, copies of orders, instructions, air photographs or plans of our trenches which might be of use to the enemy in the event of the documents falling into his hands.

(4) PRISONERS OF WAR.
    Instructions for the collection and disposal of prisoners of war have been issued as a separate memorandum.

(5) CONTROL POSTS.
    (1) Blocking posts.
        The following Blocking Posts are in position:-
        RIVER LAWE
        (a) Bridge X 13 d 7.9..   ...   1 N.C.O. & 5 men.
        (b) Bridge X 8 c 4.2.... ...   1 N.C.O. & 5 men.
        (c) Bridge X 8 Central.. ...   1 N.C.O. & 5 men.
        (d) Bridge X 3 a. ...   ...   1 N.C.O. & 5 men.
        The duty of these posts is to prevent civilians getting East of the Line.
    (ii) Stragglers Posts.
        The following Stragglers Posts will be detailed by A.P.M. from troops allotted to him for the purpose:-
                Road Junction (a) F 4 b 5.2.
                    ,,   ,,   (b) X 29 a 1.5.
                    ,,   ,,   (c) X 17 c 7.7.
        The duties of these posts will be as follows:-
        (i) To prevent any man from proceeding West of the Line of Posts unless on duty or provided with a pass.
        (ii) To collect stragglers and send them back to Brigade Headquarters where they will be reorganized and returned to units under Police arrangements.

(iii) <u>Traffic Control Posts.</u>

The following Traffic Control Posts have been detailed:-

(a) Road Junction F 5 b 5.1
(b) ,, ,, X 20 b 8.1.
(c) ,, ,, X 21 a 9.9.
(d) ,, ,, X 16 d 3.9.
(e) ,, ,, X 14 b 8.7.

No 3 Platoon

Special orders and traffic circuit maps have been issued to these posts by the A.P.M.

(6) <u>DEPOTS OF R.E. STORES.</u>

Depots have been established as under:-

<u>IND I.</u>
    Advanced depots at
        GRENADIER JUNCTION (with Fire Trench)
        FIFE JUNCTION.
        STUART JUNCTION.
        BARNTON JUNCTION.
    Intermediate depots at
        H.Q. IND I (a).
        H.Q. IND I (b).
    Reserve Depots at
        House 33 LE PLANTIN.
        House 15 (entrance to STUART Trench)
        FESTUBERT CHURCH.

<u>IND II.</u>
    Advanced depots at
        Junction of PIONEER Road and RICHMOND TRENCH.
        Crossing of SHETLAND TRENCH over QUINQUE RUE.
        Junction of FUNNEL and RICHMOND.
    Main Reserve at
        INDIAN VILLAGE.

(7) <u>SANDBAGS.</u>

The sandbags to be carried by men of Infantry and R.E. Companies will be drawn through the R.E. Companies attached to Brigades. The number of sandbags to be carried will be made up to 2 per man.

(8) <u>MEDICAL ARRANGEMENTS.</u>

Aid Posts:-
    A.1.d.5.0.
    A.2.a.5.4.
    S.25.d.3.8.
    S.21.a.3.7.
    S.20.b.6.9.
    S.14.c.8.8.
Advanced Dressing Stations:-
    F.5.b.4.4.
    X.18.d.2.4.
    X.11.b.3.3.
    S.14.c.8.8.
Main Dressing Stations:-
    59th Field Ambulance... MESPLAUX.
    58th ,, ,, ... EGLISE.
    57th ,, ,, ... BOIS DE PACAUT.
        LOCON (Oilcake Factory).

(9). WOUNDED HORSE COLLECTING STATION.

An advanced collecting post of No.31 Mobile Veterinary Section for sick and wounded horses will be at LES FACONS X 15.c.6.8. The injured horses will be taken over there by the M.V.S. and the conducting parties will return immediately to their units.

A veterinary officer will be on duty there and his assistance can be obtained by units having no veterinary officer of their own.

A.C.Bucker

22-9-1915.

Lieutenant-Colonel, G.S.,
19th Division.

Secret.

19th Division.

Artillery arrangements for support of attack.

IND. I. Artillery Group and "L"/Battery, 89th F.A. Brigade.

Time	Units	Guns	Task	Ammunition
0. - 0.10.	5 Batteries.	18-pdrs.	Alternate batteries on front and second line trenches and communication trenches between them ("B"/88 taking 2nd line trench, "L"/87 front line trench).	150 rounds Shrapnel. 72 rounds H.E. (on 2nd line).
0. - 0.20.	One Battery. "D"/89	4.5 How.	One Section on houses S.27.d.3.3. S.27.d.3.5. One Section Work S.28.d.5.6.	40 rounds H.E.
At 0.10.	5 Batteries.	18-pdrs.	All Batteries engaging front line trench commence to lift to 2nd line commencing from the right till at 0.20, all on 2nd line trench except "L"/87 which switches on to front line trench in A.3.a.	200 rounds Shrapnel.
0.20. till stopped by seeing our advance commence, message or Signal Rocket from 58th Inf. Bde. Report Centre.	One Battery "L"/87	18-pdrs.	On front line trench in A.3.a.	100 rounds Shrapnel.
On seeing commencement of attack of 58th Inf.Bde.or by Signal Rocket or message.	One Battery "C"/87		Forms Barrage on Communication trench S.27.c.8.2. - S.27.d.4.1.	100 rounds Shrapnel.

XIXth DIVISIONAL ARTILLERY.

Arrangements for support

of

2nd DIVISION.

---

0. - 0.15.	One Battery	"A"/89	4.5 How.	Houses. (to be engaged in the following order):-
				1. A.3.d.2.2. (8 rounds)
				2. A.3.d.2.4. (13 rounds)
				3. A.3.d.7.4. (8 rounds)
				4. A.3.d.9.5. (8 rounds) 40 rounds H.E.
0. - 0.15.	One Battery.	"A"/87th	18-pdr.	Front and support trenches on front A.3.d.1.1. - A.3.d.0.5.
0.15. - 0.20.	One "B"Battery	"A"/87th	18-pdr.	Communication trench A.3.d.8.6. - A.4.c.2.8. 120 rounds Shrapnel.

S E C R E T.

A. A. Goschen, Major R.F.A.
Brigade Major R.A., 19th Division.

0.15 - 0.30.	One Battery	"A"/89	4.5	On RUE D'OUVERT in A.3.b.	40 rounds H.E.
0.20 - 0.30.	One Battery.	"D"/89	4.5	One Section on S.27.d.1.7. One Section fire Shrapnel if opportunity offers.	20 rounds H.E. 8 rounds Shrapnel.
0.20 - 0.30.	4 Batteries.		18-pdrs.	RUE D'OUVERT IN A.3.b. and new trench A.4.a.0.3 - S.27.d.7.5.	160 rounds H.E.

IND.II. Artillery Group.

0. - 0.30.	5 Batteries.	Bombardment of front and 2nd Line trenches and communication trenches on their front (not S. of S.27.b.7.1)	150 rounds Shrapnel.
30 onwards.	3 Batteries.	Bombard works S.28.a.8.3. S.22.d.3.0. S.28.b.8.8.	60 rounds H.E.
	Counter Battery.	Works in conjunction with 17th bde R.G.A.	

N.B.

The main thought in these operations is that

1. The attack will probably start in a fog, or screened by smoke, etc., therefore all shooting must be done by previous registration.

2. The 2nd Division attack will reach CHLE. St. ROCH at 0.30., and our 58th Brigade attack will be launched when the 2nd Division reach A.9.b.0.9 (A.9.b.0.9.) probably about 20, when rockets will be fired.

Divisional Cyclists

Copy No. 15

Additions and Amendments to Divisional Order No.9.

The following amendments and additions are made to 19th Division Order No.9 of 22nd September 1915 to comply with the latest instructions received.

1. **GAS PRECAUTIONS.**

    Cancel the last sub para. of Para.4 (a) and substitute the amended instructions issued under G.A.85 of 22nd instant.

2. **SIGNAL FOR ATTACK BY 58TH BDE.**

    The signal for the attack by the 58th Bde. will be a sheaf of rockets of mixed colours fired from 58th Advanced Bde. Headquarters.

3. **COMMUNICATION TRENCHES FOR FORWARD AND BACK TRAFFIC.**

    The communication Trenches for forward and back traffic in the Section held by 56th Bde. are as follows:-

    Forward. CADBURY, ROPE, ARGYLL and LOTHIAN Trenches.

    Back.   FUNNEL, SHETLAND and PIONEER Trenches.

4. **AMMUNITION RESERVES.**

    The Reserves of S.A.A. and Grenades are stored at the following points:-

    58th Brigade. S.A.A.

    Battalion Reserves - distributed along the trenches.
    Machine-Gun   ,, - LEES KEEP, GOLDNEY'S KEEP and ESTAMINET CORNER.
    Brigade Reserve   - ESTAMINET CORNER and LE HAMEL.

    56th Brigade. S.A.A.

    Battalion Reserves - distributed in Fire, Support, and Reserve trenches.
    Machine-Gun   ,, - KINKROO, MARSDEN, ROPE, TUBE STATION, WATERS and FALLEN TREE KEEPS, and in CHOCOLATE and DEAD COW POSTS.
    Brigade Reserve.   - Brigade Headquarters.

    58th Brigade. Grenades.- Junction of BARNTON ROAD with Old British Line.

    56th Brigade. Grenades.- DEAD COW Bomb Store.

H.Q.19th Division,
24th September 1915.

Lieutenant-Colonel, G.S.,
19th Division.

(Issued to all recipients of Divisional Order No.9.)

Copy No. 15

19th Division Order No. 9.

22nd September 1915.

References to 1/40,000 Combined Sheet, BETHUNE,
Corps Trench Map,
and Trench Maps 36 S W 3 and 36 c N.W.1.

Information	1.	The 1st Army will assume the offensive (as indicated in preliminary instructions issued to those concerned) on 25th September, the Corps South of the LA BASSEE Canal advancing eastwards to the line PONT-A-VENDIN --- BEAUVIN; action of Corps North of Canal being as previously described, if weather conditions are favourable for a gas attack.

The Meerut Divn. will explode a mine 2 minutes before Zero. (Instructions as to time-table and other details of gas and smoke attacks are issued herewith, G.A. 80/5.)

Intention	2.	The 19th Division will take part in the offensive:-

(a) By diverting the enemy's attention from the main offensive by a feint attack on 23rd inst., and, if weather conditions permit, putting up a smoke cloud all along its front at the time of the assault. Instructions as to these have already been issued.
(b) If the weather is favourable, by co-operating with the attack by 2nd Division on its right.
(c) By taking advantage of any weakening in the enemy's resistance to push forward in the general direction VIOLAINES --- SALOME.

Bombardment	3.	The deliberate artillery bombardment which began yesterday will be continued day and night until the time of attack, under instructions already issued.
58th Bde.	4.	(a) 58th Bde. will prepare to attack in co-operation with the attack by 2nd Division, in accordance with the following plan, submitted by G.O.C. 58th Bde. and approved :-

As soon as the advance of 58th Bde. is made possible by the progress of the attack of the Brigade on its right, the signal to advance (a sheaf of rockets fired from the Advanced Report Centre 58th Bde.) will be given by the Brigadier. The 58th Bde. will thereupon attack, on the front A 3 d 1.2. to A 3 a 8.4. Its first objective will be the support trench running from A 3 d 5.2. to A 3 b 4.6. This first objective will be consolidated by the two leading battalions as soon as gained. The attack on the second objective, the trench running from A 4 c 4.6. to A 3 b 7.7½, will be carried out by the two supporting battalions, and the line consolidated when captured.

As soon as the Brigade of 2nd Divn. on the right has reached A 9 b 0.9. a right flanking party of 100 men 9/R.W.F., with 1 platoon of grenadiers and 4 machine-guns, will advance under cover of the left flank of the Brigade on the right, and will enfilade the enemy's lines to the northward in front of the attack by the rest of 58th Bde.

One company of each of the supporting battalions will hold the trenches and keeps occupied by 58th Bde.

On.

On the night of 24/25th inst., the two leading battalions will move up into the firing and support trenches, the supporting battalions into the neighbourhood of the Old British Line; move to be completed by 4 a.m. As the leading battalions move forward to attack, the supporting battalions take their places.

The dividing line between battalions will be a line running east from FIFE ROAD. This line and the lines of advance of the flanks of the Brigade should be marked on the ground with sandbags as far forward as possible before the morning of the assault.

The communication trenches to be used are :-
Right Section of attack - COLDSTREAM ROAD (No.5)
         - FIFE ROAD   (No.7)
Left ,, ,, ,, - STUART ROAD
         - BARNTON ROAD

All the above will be available for forward movement until the attack is launched. After that FIFE ROAD and BARNTON ROAD will be reserved for rearward communication and evacuation of wounded.

Lanes through the wire between Old British Line and firing trench will be cut to ensure free movement across the open in case of necessity; lanes through the wire in front of our front line will be cut on the night of 24/25th inst.

Vermorel sprayers available with 58th Bde. will be distributed in front trench where cylinders have been installed. Sprayers will be taken forward with the attack to clear hostile trenches where required for occupation and consolidation by us.

All ranks of 58th Brigade who are likely to enter the zone covered by gas will wear their smoke-helmets with vizor up. Caps will be carried. After the zone of gas has been passed the helmets can be removed, but must be carefully preserved and carried, not thrown away.

(b) The garrisons or guards furnished by the 58th Bde. at

LE PLANTIN EAST	(15 men)
FESTUBERT EAST	(20 men)
LE PLANTIN	(50 men)
FESTUBERT	(40 men)
TUNING FORK WEST	(4 men)
MARAIS EAST	(4 men)
ROUTE A	(4 men)

will be relieved by 5/S.W.B. on the evening of 23rd inst. The other caretaking guards furnished by 58th Bde. at posts will be temporarily withdrawn at the same time.

56th Bde. 5. The battalion of 56th Bde. in Divisional Reserve will be brought up to the area between CAILLOUX and RUE DE L'EPINETTE NORTH posts inclusive, east of the RUE DE L'EPINETTE and west of INDIAN VILLAGE, on the night of 24/25th inst. As much use as possible will be made of existing works and trenches to provide cover from artillery fire for this battalion. In case of urgent tactical necessity this battalion can be used as Brigade Reserve by reference to Divisional Headquarters.

Except to gain cover as above in the works included in the area mentioned, the garrisons of posts held by this battalion will not be increased.

The rôle of the 56th Bde. will at first be defensive; but as the offensive operations elsewhere progress every effort must be made to detect signs of weakening on the

part

part of the enemy, and the Brigade must be ready to take immediate advantage of any retirement of the enemy on its front to press forward on the left of 58th Bde.

57th Bde. 6. The 57th Bde., in Army Reserve, will move on the evening of 24th inst. to the area LE HAMEL --- LES GLATIGNIES --- X 19 b 7.8. --- X 20 c 8.3, and will remain in readiness for immediate movement. The march to the area will not begin before 7 p.m.

Divl. Artillery. 7. The Divl. Artillery will support the attack of 58th Bde. in accordance with the attached table, Appendix I. All preparations will be made for a subsequent advance, including the carrying of material for crossing trenches and ditches. In the event of an advance the 86th Bde.R.F.A. will probably be affiliated to 58th Bde., and the 88th Bde.R.F.A. to 56th Bde.; should the 57th Bde. be operating with the rest of the Division later, the 87th Bde.R.F.A. will probably be affiliated to it.

Divl. Engineers. 8.
(a) 94th Fld.Coy.R.E. is allotted to the front at present occupied by 58th Bde. One section will accompany that Bde. in the assault, in rear of the leading battalions; the remainder will be under orders of C.R.E., moving into the "Intermediate Line" when that is vacated by 58th Bde. Route, road junctions X 13 d 1.9. --- X 29 a 1.5.
(b) 82nd Fld.Coy.R.E. is allotted to the front now occupied by 53th Bde., under the orders of C.R.E.; one section will be, as heretofore, at the disposal of 56th Bde. if required.
(c) 81st Fld.Coy.R.E. will be in Divisional Reserve at LE TOURET; two sections, with one company 5/S.W.B. attached, are earmarked for clearing roads if the Division advances.
(d) Depots of R.E.Stores are given in separate instructions issued herewith, G.A.80/8.

5/S.W.B. (Pioneers) 9. The 5/S.W.B. will furnish the guards and garrisons mentioned in para.4(b) above.
One company is earmarked for repair of roads with 81st Fld.Coy.R.E., under the C.R.E., in the event of a general advance, and will remain at LE TOURET.
The remainder will be in Divisional Reserve about the TUNING FORK, and will be prepared either to furnish tactical support where and when required, or to open up 3 new communication trenches up to the hostile front line, when captured -
   (i) From the neighbourhood of A 3 c 2.3. towards A 3 d 1.2.
   (ii) From THE LOOP towards A 3 d 0.6.
   (iii) From front end of FIFE ROAD towards A 3 a 9.2.
Necessary moves to take place on evening of 24th inst. after 7 p.m.

Trench Mortar Batteries. 10. Trench Mortar Batteries will remain affiliated to the Brigades they are now with, and will be employed as necessary for consolidation of positions gained, &c., under the orders of Brigadiers, if ammunition arrives for them.

Divl. Mounted Troops.	11.	The Divl. Squadron and Divl. Cyclist Coy. will be temporarily detailed for duties in connection with control posts, bridge guards, salvage, and prisoners, vide separate instructions issued herewith. They will, however, be prepared to move forward when called upon for tactical employment at a later stage, in the event of a general advance. The Divl. Squadron will furnish 1 N.C.O. and 8 men and the Divl. Cyclist Coy. 4 N.C.O's and 30 men for duty with Divisional H.Q. when the Advanced Divisional Report Centre is opened. The present H.Q. Guard at LOCON will form part of this party.
Machine-guns.	12.	Instructions for the employment of machine-guns (a) in co-operation with the artillery in the preliminary bombardment have already been issued. (b) in support of the assault will be issued later.
Medical Arrangements.	13.	The medical arrangements are shown separately, in the instructions issued herewith, G.A.80/8.
Distinguishing Flags.	14.	Distinguishing flags, on the scale of 2 per company, are being issued to the Division; they are 3' x 2'3", with two staves, rear face yellow with red St. Andrew's Cross, front face khaki; those for Lahore Division are yellow, with black central vertical stripe; for 2nd Divn. yellow, reverse side khaki; about the same size as ours. They will be used to assist in showing the localities reached by our troops.

Report Centres	15.	Advanced Report Centres will be opened at 4 p.m. 24th inst:-
		    58th Bde. -- WELSH CHAPEL, A 1 d 6.9.
		    53th Bde. -- RUE DE CAILLOUX, S 20 c 5.2.
		    19th Divn. -- LOISNE, X 28 a 8.8.

Alternative Action.	16.	If the weather conditions do not permit of gas being used on the morning of the 25th, and circumstances do not admit of offensive operations being postponed, the attack by the Meerut Divn. is to be carried out, the mine being exploded at 4-57 a.m., and the assault taking place at 5 a.m.; but there will be no attack North of the Canal by the 2nd Divn. In this case action by the 19th Divn. must be limited to taking advantage of any favourable results of attacks to North and South; every effort being made to discover any weakening in the enemy's resistance, and all preparations being made for advance.

A.Butler

Lieutenant-Colonel.
General Staff.

Issued at 6-45 p.m.

Copies to:-

File	Divl. Cavalry.
War Diary	Divl. Cyclists.
G.O.C.	5th S. Wales Borderers.
G.S.	Divl. Train.
A.A.&Q.M.G.	M.M.G. Battery.
G.O.C., R.A.	A.D.M.S.
C.R.E.	Indian Corps.
56th Infantry Brigade.	Lahore Division.
57th ,, ,,	Meerut Division.
58th ,, ,,	Divl. Signal Coy.
	2nd Division.

O.C. 9th Div Cyclists

SECRET.   INSTRUCTIONS re CLEARING of BATTLEFIELD.   A. No. 3.

19th Division. /63/Z.

1. The clearing of a battlefield may be divided into 4 headings:-

    A. Evacuation of wounded.
    B. Collection and disposal of prisoners of war.
    C. Burial of the dead.
    D. Collection and disposal of R.E. material, all war material, equipment, supplies, etc.

---

2. A. Medical arrangements for the evacuation of wounded -

    1. Advanced Dressing Stations will be at
        F.5a.5.0.
        X.11.b.3.3.

    2. Main Dressing Stations will be at

        59th Field Ambulance, MESPLAUX.
        58th   -do-   EGLISE.
        57TH   -do-   BOIS DE PACAUT.
                                          LOCON.

3. B. C. D.   General Arrangements -

The Divisional Squadron and Divisional Cyclists, assisted by the Salvage Co., will perform all duties in connection with (1) Disposal of Prisoners, (2) burial of the dead, (3) collection and disposal of war material, until they are required for duty as mounted troops for the advance.

Duty.	Troops available.	Reports to.	At what place.	Date.
Clearing Battlefield.	Divl. Squad. (less 2 troops), Divl. Cyclists (4 platoons). Salvage Coy.	D.A.A. & Q.M.G.,	Notified by wire.	
Prisoners' escort to LOCON.	½ platoon Cyclists.	A.P.M.	LE TOURET.	
Prisoners' guard & escort at LOCON.	2 troops Divl. Squadron.	Major INGHAM, D.H.Q.	LOCON.	

4. B. Separate instructions have been issued regarding the collection and disposal of prisoners of war.

5. C. Burial of the dead.

If circumstances permit, the dead will be collected and taken from the battlefield by tram and stretcher to cemeteries at LE TOURET, FESTUBERT, BROWNS ROAD, RUE des BERCEAUX.

Bodies will be taken from Field Ambulances to LOCON Cemetery.

Where circumstances do not permit of bodies being taken to the cemeteries certain easily distinguishable spots will be selected as burial places.

In this respect attention is drawn to G.R.Os 423, 913, 624, 670 in "Extracts from General Routine Orders 1915."

6. D. <u>COLLECTION AND DISPOSAL OF ALL WAR MATERIAL, EQUIPMENT, SUPPLIES, ETC</u>

The existing Salvage Company will be the nucleus of the Collecting Party assisted by Divl. Squadron & Divl. Cyclist Company and further expanded by Civil labour if it is found necessary. The whole under the command of Major Ingham, Divl. Squadron.

7. <u>Depots</u> exist as shown on attached sketch at 1, 2, 3, 4, 5, 6, as follows:-

   1. Main Ordnance Depot.
   2. Main R.E. Depot.
   3.4.5. Sub Depots R.E.
   6. Bomb Store.

Depots for Battalion store will be formed at each Bn. H.Qrs. vide map, under supervision of Quartermasters concerned. 1 man per Coy. will be left in charge of battalion stores.

<u>R.E. Depots</u>. A representative of the R.E. will be left in charge at each R.E. sub depot.

The stores will not be moved until orders to this effect are given.

8. <u>Intermediate Collecting Stations</u> will be formed at F.5.b.4.2. (A), ~~X.17.c.6.1.~~ (B), Road junction RUE de CAILLAUX S.25.b. (C), S.7.d.2.3. (D). C.5.B.d.5.9

The Central Collecting Station will be at LOCON, X 7 central.

Grenades and bombs will not be moved.

All material and stores in the trenches and in depots and keeps (except grenades and bombs) will be collected and taken to intermediate Collecting Stations at A, B, C, D as above.

They will be divided into 2 categories,

  (1). Stores to be sent forward, viz, picks, shovels, sandbags, wire, ammunitions greatcoats, etc.

  (2). Stores to be sent back, rifles, equipment, clothing, rations

Articles in (1) will be stored in the intermediate Collecting Station till they can be sent forward.

Articles under (2) will be evacuated to Main Store at LOCON on carts detailed for the purpose. Localities where stores will be found are (1) Trenches, (2) Redoubts, (3) Battalion Depots, (4) Existing Depots. The N.C.O. at each intermediate Collecting Station will keep a list of the articles stored there, ~~vide attached pro forma.~~

9. The area to be cleared is divided into two sections corresponding to the fronts now held by Brigades:-

        Ind. 1 Section.
        Ind. 2 Section.

10. TROOPS DETAILED FOR THE WORK.

        Divisional Squadron (Yorkshire Dragoons).
        Divisional Cyclist Company.
        Salvage Coy.

ALLOTMENT OF MEN, etc.

    1 Officer & 30 men, Divl. Squadron.)
    1 Officer & 40 men, Divl. Cyclists.) IND. 1.
    N.C.O. & 15 men, Salvage Coy.)

    1 Officer & 30 men, Divl. Squadron)
    1 Officer & 40 men, Divl. Cyclists.) IND. 2.
    1 N.C.O. & 15 Men, Salvage Coy.)

1 N.C.O. & 9 men at each intermediate Collecting Station.

1. N.C.O. & 20 men Divl. Squadron at Central Collecting Station, LOCON.

The D.A.D.O.S. will detail two Ordnance representatives to assist in listing the articles at LOCON.

11. A detailed list of local transport available for hire is attached. Carts are allotted as follows:-

    A)
    B) IND. 1   10 to 15 carts.

    C)
    D) IND. 2.   10 to 15 carts.

Major Ingham will arrange to requisition these carts as required. Requisitions to be filled in with date and time and place at which required and sent to O.C. Divl. Train to arrange delivery.

D.H.Q.,   P.M. Davies, Lieut-Colonel,
21/9/15.   A.A. & Q.M.G., 19th Division.

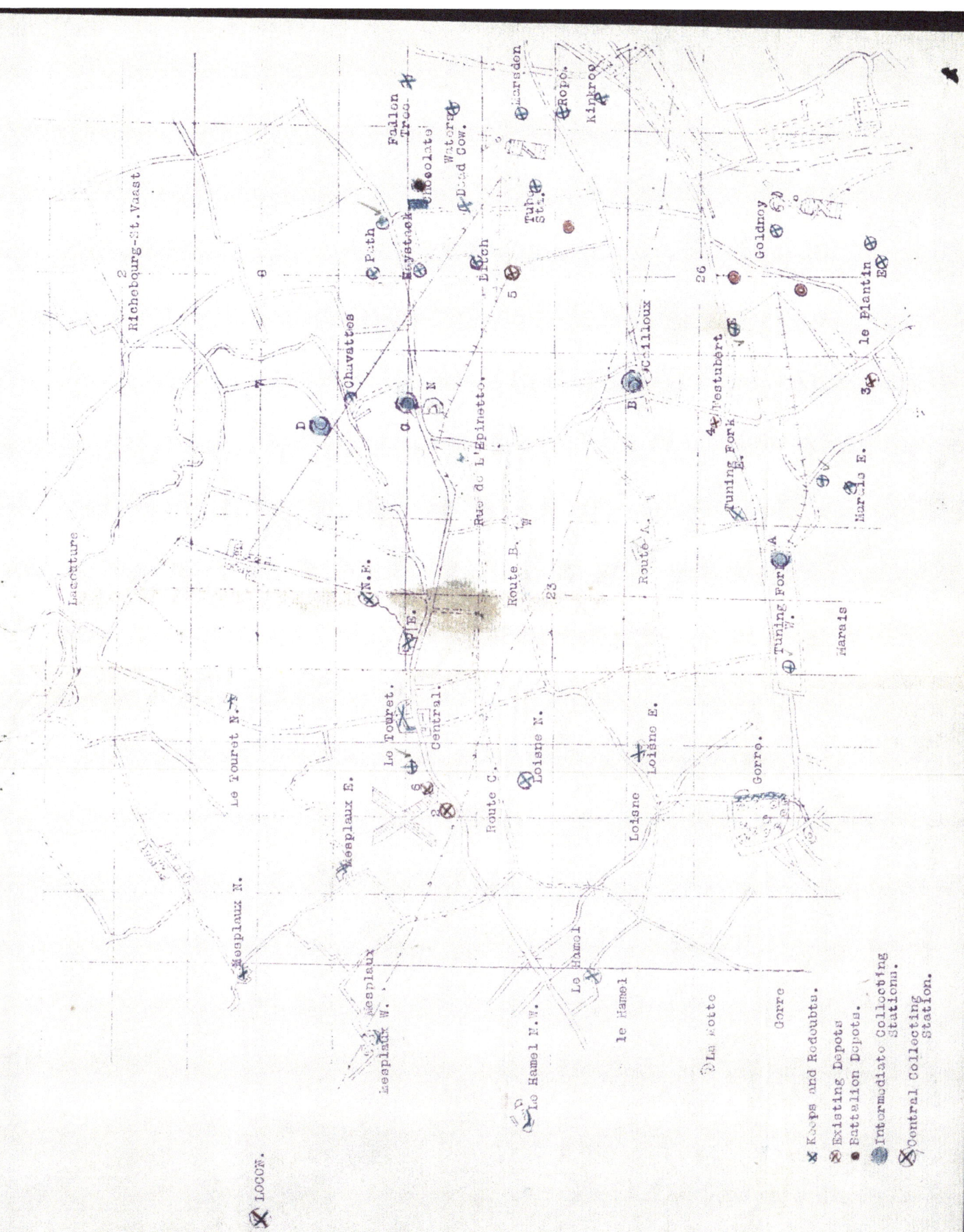

121/7517

19ᵗʰ Burmin

19ᵗʰ Burmh: Cycl: Coy:
Vol: 3

Oct 15

Army Form C. 2118

WAR DIARY
or
INTELLIGENCE SUMMARY
(Erase heading not required.)

Confidential

War Diary
of
19th Division Cyclist Company
From Oct. 4th 1915. To Oct. 31st 1915.

(Volume 3)

WAR DIARY
or
INTELLIGENCE SUMMARY Part Sheet No 8.

Army Form C. 2118

Place	Date	Hour	Summary of Events and Information	Remarks and references to Appendices
HINGETTE	1/10/15		Weather wet cold. Wind from N.W. O/oo notes 299/15 from OC 19 DCC to OPOR 19 Div. "So Him and posted S/H's stragglers posts and road control posts found by this Unit evening in area. He proposes escort having returned 9 Homefeld if possible the stragglers' posts which he doing likewise now. Should this not be the case would you have him any objection at the end of this week to my relieving them with others now of the Unit am.	
	2/10/15		Weather fine rainy. Wire from M.Y. Coln. O/oo dated 2/10/15 from DHQ "Reconnaître PACAUT (or Billet Tral and report result with own Squadron also going there." OC 2CC 9/13 dates 9/9/15 "Have reconnaître billets at PACAUT area. Room there for this unit but not for both area understand." Squadron Rates made arrangements of billet close by.	
	3/10/15		Weather fine rainy cold. Moved into billets at PACAUT about point Q23 c 39 / n2/3 96 (Carlow) (BETHUNE)	

WAR DIARY or INTELLIGENCE SUMMARY

Army Form C. 2118

Sheet No. 9.

Place	Date	Hour	Summary of Events and Information	Remarks and references to Appendices
ZELOBES PACAUT	4/10/15		O/27 dated 4/10/15 from O.C. 19. D.C.C. to 19. D.H.Q. concerning relief of Control and Slinghim H.Os furnished by this Unit under APM 19. Div: and stating that they needed to be relieved. A/681 dated 5/10/15 from 19. D.H.Q. to O.C. D.C.C. "you may take steps to relieve from men on all H.Os as soon as convenient to you".	J.C.A.S.
	5/10/15		nil	J.C.A.S.
	6/10/15		No. 5464. Private Smith W. unearthed to No. 33. ST. VENANT. Received 19. Division Order. No. 12 dated 6/10/15 notifying that on account of the G.O.C. 7th Bde. revolting to the Indian Corps on 7th October, for relief of 7th Div: an increase in the Div: billeting area has consequently been made. Under this plan the M.D.C.C. move to Lillers.	J.C.A.S.
ZELOBES	7/10/15		ZELOBES. Times of arrival and positions of H.Q. of units to be reported to D.H.Q. O/33 dated 7/10/15 from O.C. M.D.C.C. to 19. D.H.Q. "Headquarters this company situated at R.26.a.7.5. (Combined Chief - BETHUNE). c/dated 7/10/15 from Camp Commandant 19. Div: to M.D.C.C. "H.Q. guard and Trench guides — 31st inst: forward reply if no round-up for including them in my payment." O/35 dated 5/10/15 from O.C. A/C Commandant 19. Div: "Will pay me if this company forming H.Q. guard once during the course of each such arrangements have been made to try have many at 3 dated today and should have done this earlier but various men have made it difficult."	J.C.A.S.
	8/10/15		GA.O/2 from 19. D.H.Q. dated 8/10/15 in information and guidance in the event of a local battle attack, at the other houses of Battle positions being most; action to take in course of readiness of the Divisional Cavalry and Cyclists will assemble at their places has to devoting such to advanced Batt:s for the completion of the Vay's move they will "probably be called on to VIEILLE CHAPELLE. Advanced report centre for 19. Div. will "be at white house VIEILLE CHAPELLE."	J.C.A.S.

WAR DIARY
or
INTELLIGENCE SUMMARY

Army Form C. 2118

Sheet No. 10.

Place	Date	Hour	Summary of Events and Information	Remarks and references to Appendices
ZELOBES	9/10/15		Return of self-inflicted wounds called for by D.A.G. Reference D.R.O. No. 253.	JC/sl
	10/10/15		O/39 dated 10/10/15 from H.Q. 19.D.C.C. G.R.E. 19. Div. Cav.: "We have now to continue cleaning out the ditches in the forward area which are exceptionally wet and slimey & have some ground to are not class engaged in this work could you let us have them and if however from we can we have some of them."	JC/sl
	11/10/15			JC/sl
	12/10/15		A/26 dated 12/10/15 from 19. DHQ. to H.Q. 19.C.C.: "Detail 4 NCOs + 16 men for duty in pads 5 to be taken near Pitres LAHORE Division Hdqrs and they should meet the A.P.M. 19. Division at the bridge over canal at FOSSE at 2.30 p.m. today and be returned by our own advanced M.Cyclists, repeated A.P.M." Our dated 12/10/15 from O.C. 19.D.C.C. to 19.DHQ. "All the company available are working in the forward area on the ditches there are no sundry men for H.Q. 4 NCOs and 16 men required."	JC/sl
	13/10/15		Return of Railway wounds (ADs 205, 206) called for by 19 DHQ. M.6430 RCP Host M&B forms in reinforcements from 27 bnh Field Reput Rouen Sun	JC/sl
	14/10/15			JC/sl
FOSSE	15/10/15		O/46 dated 15/10/15 from H.Q. 19 D.C.C. to O.C. Signals, 19 DHQ. "Kindly note H.Q. 7 this Company moves today at 11 a.m. to R. 16.C.7.5. (Combined sheet = BETHUNE) and will so advise (i.e "G-A") Shall I send in further map sheet of the area."	JC/sl

WAR DIARY or INTELLIGENCE SUMMARY

Army Form C. 2118

Sheet No. 71.

Place	Date	Hour	Summary of Events and Information	Remarks and references to Appendices
FOSSE	15/10/15		Weather dull and misty. No rain.	
	16/10/15		Weather fine. 48 NCOs & Men placed under quarantine by A.D.M.S. — one spotted case of Spotted fever.	
	17/10/15		Weather dull and misty. No rain. Arrival from R.B. No. 5008 Private Johnson evacuated to No. 33. C.C. Station ST. VENANT.	
	18/10/15		Weather fine. Lieut SON HOGBEN Transferred to 81st Field Coy R.E. for duty temporarily.	
	19/10/15		Work of clearing River LOISNE continues with very few men left. 2 Lieut R.S. TALBOT Transferred to 82nd Field Co. R.E. for duty temporarily. Captain J.C.S. WHITTUCK gone on HAVRE. Major Comr. No. 6493 Pte Oxley, S. Jones as a reinforcement from S.H.T. Base Depot, HINGETTE. 2 Lieut G.A. MORRIS join up. Units previously overseas at HINGETTE for 20 mts.	
	20/10/15		Weather fine. All cars. Work on LOISNE continues. All men taken out of quarantine by order A.D.M.S. Indian Corps Baths at LESTREM allotted to Coy for the afternoon.	
HINGETTE	21/10/15		Coy move to HINGETTE as arranged — WILL 2.8 (Combined Sheet 36) N18th Division (the one front previously occupied. RUNS - LOCON ARM Road Lodge pts changed from No. 4 Stationary Hospital ARCQUES. 9646 Pte Taylor J. join as reinforcement from No 4 Stationary Hospital ARCQUES.	

WAR DIARY or INTELLIGENCE SUMMARY

Army Form C. 2118

Sheet No 12

Place	Date	Hour	Summary of Events and Information	Remarks and references to Appendices
HINGETTE	23/10/15		Weather dry hot cold. Work continued on R. LOISNE	fair
	24/10/15		Coll. at unity. 1 Sergeant on leave. No 5784 Pte Ashmore B (9/10/15) and No 3885 LCpl Gurlott to (17/10/15) evacuated to MEERUT C.C. Stn. No 3199 Pte Corbin (and No 6490 Pte Hooper J.S. join as re-inforcements from No 5 Inf Base, HAVRE. Work in forward area is now carried out as follows. Proposal to form a Theatrical Troupe Pte called the "Involved Ladies" Move off at 8:30 am with a Cheese & cart return to billets for dinner at 3:45 pm	fair
	24/10/15		Weather very hot. 1 Corporal goes on leave.	fair
	25/10/15		Too wet to go into forward area. Roads in an appalling condition	fair
	26/10/15		Fine 6 p.m. Road Control Posts relieves. Work on R. LOISNE continued by the RUE DU BOIS. To RUE DU BOIS was shelled between 1 & 2:30 pm. The Coy had to obtain cover for some time	fair
	27/10/15		very hot. Afternoon - inspection rations "table."	fair
	28/10/15		Work continued in forward area. Relieved at 1 pm too hot to continue	fair
	29/10/15		Pte Harbertson R. No 40324 join us reinforcement from No 19 Inf Base Depot Staff ETAPLES A large main ditch started in connection with the drainage system - from No 7 & 85 (Shut St (continued) into the stream running from Estaminet Corner to Refuges at X 7d 5a 5pm ESTAMINET CORNER R. LOISNE	fair

WAR DIARY
INTELLIGENCE SUMMARY

Army Form C. 2118

Sheet No. 13.

Place	Date	Hour	Summary of Events and Information	Remarks and references to Appendices
HINGETTE	30/9/15		Work continued on new ditch and finishes on R. LOISNE. Captain J.S. WHITTUCK, R.E. 3rd Army, near Amiens. to No 253 Tunnelling Co. R.E. rt report RCRE 3rd Army, near Amiens.	Seconded
	31/9/15	10.30 a.m	Wet. Parade for divine service on Coy parade ground with Air Squadron. "Stables" at 10.30 a.m. 650 Dts Army C. evacuates spot de HILLERS (27/9/15).	

Charles F. Smith Captain
OC 4th R. Division Cyclist Coy

SECRET. G.A.52/2.

O.C. Divl.Cavalry.
  Divl.Cyclists.
H.Q. 56th Infantry Brigade.
     57th   ,,   ,,
     58th   ,,   ,,
O.C. 5th South Wales Borderers.
****

Reference to 1/40,000 Combined Sheet, BETHUNE.

On the supposition that the Division remains for some time in its present area, the following will be included in the Defence Scheme for the area; and is now issued for information and guidance in the event of a local hostile attack, on the order "Move to battle positions" being issued.

x   x   x   x   x   x

ACTION OF TROOPS IN RESERVE.

1. Battalions in Brigade Reserve will concentrate forward under the orders of G.Os.C. Brigades in front line.

2. Battalions in Divisional Reserve will move as follows:-
   (a) Battalion of Brigade in Ind III, from LES LOBES, will form up about X 17 a and c.
       Route. By road (not shown on map) to trestle bridge at PASSLLE., X 3 a, and thence by road-junctions X 3 c 9.0., X 8 b 8.3., X 15 b 2.7., and X 15 d 3.9.
   (b) Battalion of Brigade in Ind IV, from VIEILLE CHAPELLE, will form up about X 5 d,
       Route. Road from PT.LEVIS to LACOUTURE.

3. The Brigade not in front line is in Corps Reserve, and according to instructions from Indian Corps, is to move forward to the line LE TOURET -- LACOUTURE in the event of serious attack. The move, when ordered, will be carried out as follows:-
   (a) Two battalions, from about PACAUT and PARADIS, will move by the same route as laid down in 2(a) above to the neighbourhood of LE TOURET (west of LE TOURET -- LACOUTURE road).
   (b) The other two battalions and Brigade H.Q. will move via LA CIX.MARMUSE -- ZELOBES -- VIEILLE CHAPELLE to the neighbourhood of LACOUTURE, on the south of that village, and west of LE TOURET -- LACOUTURE road.
       In the event of a local hostile attack on the front held by this Division, it is probable that permission for the temporary employment of the Brigade by the Divisional Commander will be obtained. In this case also its first move will be as above.

4. The Divisional Cavalry and Cyclists will assemble at their alarm posts, sending 4 orderlies each to Advanced Divisional H.Q. On the completion of the infantry moves. they will probably be called in to VIEILLE CHAPELLE.

5. 5th S.W.B. will form up, as Divisional Reserve, near their billets at LE TOURET, clear of the roads and east of the LE TOURET -- LACOUTURE road.

REPORT CENTRES.

Advanced Report Centres will be established as follows:-

        Indian Corps   -----   LESTREM
        Meerut Division -----   LOISNE
        Lahore ,,   -----   PONT DU HEM.
        19th ,,   -----   White House, VIEILLE CHAPELLE.
        Ind III.   -----   RUE DE CAILLOUX, S 20 c 5.2.
        Ind IV.   -----   RUE DES BERCEAUX, S 8 b 3.4.

H.Q. 19th Division,
8/10/15.

Lieutenant-Colonel.
General Staff.

Copy No.

19th Division Order No 12.
****

6th October 1915.

Reference to 1/40,000 Combined Sheet, BETHUNE.

Information   1.   The 58th Bde. reverts to the Indian Corps on 7th October, on relief by 7th Divn.
     An increase in the Divisional billeting area has consequently been made.
     A movement of battalions in relief is being carried out by 57th Bde. on the night of 7th/8th October.

Moves.   2.   The following moves will take place on 7th October:-

57th Bde.   (a) The battalion of 57th Bde. moving into Divisional Reserve will march into billets at VIEILLE CHAPELLE instead of ZELOBES.

Artillery.   (b) 87th Bde. R.F.A. to LES RUES DES VACHES, present billets to be clear by 4 p.m.

58th Bde.   (c) 58th Bde. on relief to billets in the area EPINETTE -- LE BOUZATEUX FME -- PACAUT -- R 19 c (exclusive of EGLISE) -- R 13 d (exclusive of road from R 13 d to EPINETTE); and about ZELOBES.

Divl. Cyclists   (d) The Divl. Cyclist Coy. to billets in ZELOBES.

Reports.   3.   Times of arrival and positions of H.Q. of Units to be reported to Divl.H.Q.

Issued at 8 p.m.

Lieutenant-Colonel.
General Staff.

Copies to:-

File	5th S.Wales Borderers.(Pnrs)
War Diary	Divl.Train.
G.O.C.	M.M.G.Battery.
G.S.	A.D.M.S.
A.A.&.Q.M.G.	Indian Corps.
G.O.C.,R.A.	Lahore Division.
C.R.E.	Meerut ,,
56th Infantry Brigade.	Divl.Signal Coy.
57th ,, ,,	7th Division.
58th ,, ,,	Divl.Cavalry.
Divl.Cyclists.	

****

SKETCH MAP
Showing German Units
Located on 30.9.

[Stamp: ORDERLY ROOM 5 OCT 1915 19TH DIV. CYCLIST CO.]

La Bassée Canal

Auchy-les-La-Bassée

Haisnes

3rd Bn 11th Bav Regt (3rd Div" II Bav Corps)
1st Bn 13th Bav Regt (3rd do. do.)
1st Bn 72nd Regt (8th do. IV Corps)
11th Res Regt of 117th Div.
15th Res Inf Regt of 2nd Guard Res Div (from Douai)
5th Bav Res Reg of 4th Div I Bav Corps
15th Res Inf Regt of 2nd Guard Res Div (from ALLENNE)
91st Res. Inf. Regt. do. do. (from DOUAI)

157th Inf. Regt of 117th Div"

77th Res. Reg. of 2nd Guard Res. Div.

Hulluch.

No Identifications
probably 56th or 57th
and Elements of other Regts

Old German Front Line

Front Line

British New Line

LOOS

Puits N°14
178th Regt 123rd Divn (from Lens)
153rd Regt 8th Divn IV Corps
93rd Reg. 8th Divn IV Corps (from Douai)
Part of 6th Regt of 7th Divn IV Corps (from Lens)
Field Coy 4th Pioneers IV Corps (from Lens)
27th Reg 7th Divn IV Corps (from Noyelles sous Lens)
165th Reg 7th Divn IV Corps
22nd Res Regt of 117th Div.
Part 157th Res Inf Regt
of 117th Div"

Double Crassier

Scale 1: 2000

19th Division Order No.11.
****

References to 1/40,000 Combined Sheet, BETHUNE,
and Corps Trench Map.

Copy

Information.   1.   The front held by Indian Corps will be readjusted
                as follows, beginning this evening:-
                    Meerut Divn. is to hold from LA BASSEE Canal
                    to ORKNEY ROAD inclusive (IND I and II).
                    19th Divn. will hold from ORKNEY ROAD exclusive
                    to VINE STREET inclusive (IND III and IV).
                    Lahore Divn. will hold from VINE STREET to
                    SUNKEN ROAD, both exclusive (IND V and VI).
                    58th Bde. has been detached to the section
                    of front S of the Canal, and attached to 7th
                    Divn.; 56th and 57th Bdes. will hold the new
                    front of 19th Division.

Distribution.   2.   19th Division will move in accordance with the
                attached March Table, details of reliefs being
                arranged between the Brigades concerned.
                    Whichever Brigade is temporarily in the vicinity
                of LE HAMEL will be for the time in Army Reserve,
                and will be ready to move at one hour's notice.

Artillery   3.   Orders as to Artillery reliefs will be issued
Relief.   shortly.

Divl.Engineers. 4.   On completion of the readjustment of the line
                81st Fld.Coy.R.E. is allotted to IND.III, and 94th
                Fld.Coy.R.E. to IND IV.

Reports.   5.   Reports to Adv.Divl.H.Q.,LOISNE until 10 a.m.
                3rd October; after that hour to FOSSE CHATEAU,
                R 15 d 3.10.

                                                Lieutenant-Colonel.
                                                General Staff.

Issued at 10 pm

Copies to:- File   5th S.Wales Borderers.(Pnrs)
             War Diary.   Divl.Train.
             G.O.C.   M.M.G.Battery.
             G.S.   A.L.M.S.
             A.A.& Q.M.G.   Indian Corps.
             G.O.C.,R.A.   Lahore Division.
             C.R.E.   Meerut   ,,
             56th Infantry Brigade.   Divl.Signal Coy.
             57th   ,,   ,,   7th Division.
             58th   ,,   ,,   Sirhind Brigade.
             DivlCavalry.   Dehra Dun ,,
             Divl. Cyclists.

                            ****

Addenda to 19th Division Order No.11.
****

2/10/15.

Artillery Reliefs.	1.	Artillery reliefs will be carried out in accordance with Instructions (No.1) by G.O.C.,R.A., 19th Divn., issued to-day to those concerned.
R.E.Moves.	2.	On 3rd October 94th Fld.Coy. moves to COUR ST.VAAST, X 5 b. 81st Fld.Coy. ,, ,, LE TOURET, X 17 a 1.0. Billets now occupied by 81st Fld.Coy. will be taken over by a Coy.S & M of Meerut Division.
Trench Mortars.	3.	No.4 Trench Mortar Battery remains attached to 57th Bde. for the present.
M.M.G.Battery.	4.	Section of M.M.G.Battery near LE PLANTIN comes back into reserve this evening, to take up a position in IND IV when that Section is taken over by 57th Bde.
Report Centres.	5.	H.Q. 58th Bde.(IND III) moves to CSE.LU RAUX at 4p.m. to-day; H.Q.57th Bde.(IND IV) to Red House, LACOUTURE, at 5 p.m. on 3rd inst.

Lieutenant-Colonel.
General Staff.

Copies to

File
War Diary.
G.O.C.
G.S.
A.A.&.Q.M.G.
G.O.C.,R.A.
G.R.E.
56th Infantry Brigade.
57th ,, ,,
58th ,, ,,
Divl.Cavalry.
Divl.Cyclists.

5th S.Wales Borderers.(Pnrs)
Divl.Train.
M.M.G.Battery.
A.D.M.S.
Indian Corps.
Lahore Division.
Meerut ,,
Divl.Signal Coy.

Date	Unit	From	To	Route	Remarks
October. night 1st/2nd	Bareilly Bde.	LA GORGUE	Trenches IND I.	--	Under instructions already issued.
	Sirhind Bde. (not including 1/Seaforths.)	Trenches IND I.	Vicinity of LE HAMEL	--	-do- 1/Seaforths remain in IND I c.
2nd	Sirhind Bde.	LE HAMEL	LA GORGUE	Bridge in X 13 d -- LOCON -- PONT RIQUEUL.	Rejoining its own Division - to be clear of road-junction at ZELOBES by 10 a.m.
	Dehra Dun Bde.	VIEILLE CHAPELLE	vicinity of LE HAMEL	ZELOBES -- LOCON -- Bridge X 13 d.	Not to pass ZELOBES road-junction before 10 a.m. and to reach LE HAMEL by noon.
	5th/S.W.Bdrs. (Pioneers)	GORRE	LE TOURET	via LOISNE	March from GORRE at 5-30 p.m.
Night 2nd/3rd	Dehra Dun Bde.	LE HAMEL	Trenches IND II	GORRE -- MARAIS -- road-junction F 6 c 3.9.	1st Seaforths come back under orders of Dehra Dun Bde.
	57th Bde.	Trenches IND II	LE HAMEL	As above	Troops of 57th Bde. in front and support trenches between ORKNEY ROAD and S 27 b 4.3½. remain there and come under the orders of Dehra Dun Bde., until relieved by 56th Bde. on night of 3rd/4th.
3rd	H.Q.19th Divn.	LOCON and LOISNE	FOSSE	--	March from road-junction X 20 b 8.1. at 2-30 p.m. Preparatory to moving into trenches. In Brigade Reserve.
	57th Bde.	LE HAMEL	2 Bns. vicinity of LE TOURET and RUE LES CHAVATTES 1Bn. to billets about LACOUTURE. 1 Bn. to billets near ZELOBES (as near LESTREM LOCON road as possible.)	Via LE TOURET. Via LE TOURET and VIEILLE CHAPELLE -- to clear GARHWAL Bde. on march.	In Divl. Reserve.

Date	Unit	From	To	Route	Remarks.
October 3rd	94th Fld.Coy R.E.	Present Billets.	Billets in new Livl. Area, to be notified later.		
	Livl.Cavalry. (Yorkshire Lgns.) Livl.Cyclists.	Present Billets	PACAUT.		
Night 3rd/4th	1 Bn.56th Bde.	Trenches in present IND III c.	About LES LOBES. (as near LESTREM — LOCOU road as possible.	Under Bde. arrangements.	Into Livl.Reserve, Batt. is RUE LES CRAVATTES becomes Bde.Reserve, IND III. 56th Bde. extends its front to the right as far as OPKNEY ROAD, exclusive, relieving the remaining detachment of 57th Bde. which rejoins its Bde.
	2 Bns. 57th Bde.	About LE TOURET and RUE LES CHAVattes.	Trenches IND IV.	Under Bde. arrangements.	1 Bn takes over the present IND III c from 56th Bde. 1 Bn. takes over from FARm CORNER exclusive to VINE STREET inclusive from Ferozepore Bde.

Battalion frontages in IND III and IV to be adjusted by Brigade Commanders, and reported to L.H.Q. Staff Captains 56th and 57th Bdes., or representatives, will meet A.A.&Q.M.G. at LOISNE at 9-30 a.m. on 2nd inst. to reconnoitre and define billeting areas.

****

Divl Cyclists

19th Division Order No.14.

Copy No.........

19th October 1915.

Reference to 1/40,000 Combined Sheet BETHUNE and Corps Trench Map.

1. Meerut Division is handing over to 28th Division, 1st Corps, the front from the LA BASSEE Canal to GRENADIER ROAD (exclusive to 28th Divn); instead of as stated in 19th Division Order No.13 of yesterday, which is now cancelled.
   The readjustment of the front held by the Indian Corps, mentioned in the above Operation Order, is therefore altered, and the 19th Division front will extend from junction of GRENADIER ROAD with the front line, at A 3 c 1.2., to PIPE Communication Trench, inclusive. The new sections on this front will be numbered IND I and IND II.

2. The relief will be carried out in accordance with the attached March Table; details being arranged between Brigades or units concerned.

3. The New Ind I Section will extend from A 3 c 1.2 to ORKNEY ROAD (inclusive).
   The present Ind III Section becomes the new Ind II, except that PIPE Communication Trench will be inclusive to it, instead of exclusive as at present.

4. Instructions with regard to artillery reliefs and responsibility for posts are being issued separately.

5. No.11 Trench Mortar Battery, on transfer from Meerut Division on 20th, will be attached to 56th Bde in the new Ind II, reporting at CSE. DU RAUX at 3 p.m.

6. Progress of reliefs will be reported to Divnl. H.Q.

7. G.Os.C Bdes in front line will take over command of their new sections on completion of reliefs.
   Bde. H.Q. will be   Ind I --- LOISNE.
                          Ind II === CSE. DU RAUX.

8. Divl. H.Q. will close at FOSSE CHATEAU at 10 a.m. on 21st inst. and will open at LOCON at the same hour.
   At that hour G.OC. 19th Division will assume command of the new Divisional Front.

Issued at 6.0 p.m.

Lieutenant-Colonel,
General Staff.

Copies to :-

File.	Divnl.Train.
War Diary.	H.M.Gun Battery.
G.O.C.	A.D.M.S.
G.S.	Indian Corps.
A.A.&.Q.M.G.	Lahore Division.
G.O.C., R.A.	Meerut "
C.R.E.	Divnl.Signal Coy.
56th Infy.Bdo.	" Cavalry.
57th " "	" Cyclists.
58th " "	28th Division.
5/S.W.Borderers.	7th Division.

MARCH-TABLE --- 19TH DIVISION.

Date.	Unit.	From Area.	To destination.	Time.	Route.	Remarks.
October 20th.	94th Fld.Coy.R.E.	COUR ST.VAAST	Billets in X 10 c.	2-30 p.m.	Bridge X 5 b 3.2.LACOUTURE -- LE TOURET road.	To be clear of its billets in COUR ST. VAAST by 2-30 p.m.
20th.	57th Bde:- M.G.Coy. Grenadier Coy	Present billets	Vicinity of LOISNE		Via LE TOURET	Time to be arranged between 57th & Garhwal Bdes.
20th.	5/S.W.B:- H.Qrs.& 1 Coy. 1 Coy.	LE TOURET. " " " "	GORRE CHATEAU. Take over posts from Dehra Dun Bde. Handle of TUNING FORK.			
20th.	58th Bde.	PARADIS area and VIEILLE CHAPELLE.	LOCON area.		Via LES LOBES.	Not to arrive in new area before 4-0 p.m.
20th.	Divl.Squadron.	LE QUENTIN.	LA PANNERIE.			
Night 20/21st.	1 Bn.57th Bde.	Trenches PIPE Communication trench to VINE STREET.	Intermediate line by ESTAMINET CORNER.		RUE DE L'EP-INETTE.	} Relieved by } Garhwal Bde. } }
	1 Bn.57th Bde.	Trenches VINE STREET.	LE HAMEL.		RUE DU BOIS.	} }
	2 Bn.57th Bde.	Bde.Reserve.	Trenches from GRENA-DIER RD (incl) to ORKNEY Road (inclusive).			Relieving Lehra Lun Bde. Times etc. to be arranged between Bdes.
	H.Qrs.57th Bde.	Present billets.	LOISNE.	On completion of relief.		
21st.	H.Qrs.19th Divn. Divl.Cyclist Coy Divl.San.Sec. Divnl.Mob.Vet.Sec	FOSSE. " " "	LOCON. W 11 b 2.8. Factory, LOCON. LOCON.			

N.B. The Battalion of 57th Brigade now garrisoning Posts and Keeps will be relieved as regards those garrisons by a Company from the Garhwal Brigade during afternoon of 20th instant.

Cyclists

Copy No. 25

19th Division Order No.13.

19th October 1915.

References to Corps Trench Map
and 1/40,000 combined sheet BETHUNE.

1. Meerut Division is handing over to 28th Division, 1st Corps, the front from the LA BASSEE Canal to THE LOOP (inclusive to 28th Divn), commencing on 19th inst. This relief to be completed by 6 a.m. 22nd inst.
   Concurrently with this relief the front held by the Indian Corps will be readjusted as follows, commencing on 19th inst :-

   <u>19th Divn.</u> from THE LOOP (exclusive) to CADBURY communication trench (exclusive). The new sections on this front will be numbered IND I and IND II.
   <u>Meerut Divn.</u> thence to the LA BASSEE road exclusive.
   <u>Lahore Divn.</u> thence to SUNKEN ROAD (exclusive).

2. The relief will be carried out in accordance with the attached March Table; details being arranged between Brigades or units concerned.

3. SHETLAND ROAD will belong to the new IND II, PIONEER ROAD to the new IND I; ARGYLE ROAD will be neutral. RICHMOND TRENCH will belong to the new IND II as far S. as its intersection with ARGYLE ROAD inclusive; RUE DE CAILLOUX, including CAILLOUX posts, will belong to IND II. *Point of division on front line will be at junction of Orchard support trench with S/side of Salient, inclusive to IND II*

4. Separate instructions will be issued regarding artillery reliefs and responsibility for posts.

5. No.11 Trench Mortar Battery, on transfer from Meerut Division on 20th, will be attached to 56th Bde, reporting at CSE. DU RAUX at 3-0 p.m.

6. Progress of reliefs will be reported to Divnl. H.Q.

7. G.Os.C. Bdes in front line will take over command of their new sections on completion of reliefs. Bde H.Q. will be - IND I -- LOISNE.
   IND II -- CSE. DU RAUX.

8. Divisional H.Q. will close at FOSSE CHATEAU at 10 a.m. on 21st inst., and will open at LOCON at the same hour. At that hour G.O.C. 19th Divn. will assume command of the new Divnl. front.

Issued at 5-15 p.m.

Lieutenant-Colonel,
General Staff.

Copies to :-
File.
War Diary.
G.O.C.
G.S.
A.A.&.Q.M.G.
G.O.C., R.A.
C.R.E.
56th Infy.Bde.
57th " "
58th " "
5/S.W.Borderers.

Divnl. Train.
M.M.Gun Battery.
A.D.M.S.
Indian Corps.
Lahore Division.
Meerut "
Divnl.Signal Coy.
" Cavalry.
" Cyclists.
28th Division.

MARCH TABLE --- 19TH DIVISION.

Date	Unit	From Area	Time	To Destination	Route	Remarks
October 20th	Portion of Battn. of 55th Bde. in Ind. III(a).	ORKNEY Road (excl.) -- to junction of ORCHARD Support Trench and South side of Salient.	by 6-0 p.m.	As directed by G.O.C. 56th Bde.	PIONEER Road	Relieved by troops from one of the Reserve Bns. 57th Bde. To be arranged between Bdes.
20th	Portion of Bn. of 57th Bde. in Ind IV(a)	PIPE Comm. Trench -- to CADBURY (excl)	by 6-0 p.m.	Intermediate Line		To be relieved by 56th Bde. as arranged between Bdes.
20th	94th Fld.Coy.R.E.	COUR ST.VAAST	2-30 p.m.	Billets in X 10 c.	Bridge X 5 b 3.2. LACOUTURE -- LE TOURET -- COUR ST. VAAST road.	To be clear of its billets in COUR ST. VAAST by 2-30 p.m.
20th	57th Bde:- M.G.Coy. Grenadier Coy}	Present billets		Vicinity of LOISNE.	Via LE TOURET.	Time to be arranged between 57th & Garhwal Bdes.
20th	5/S.W.B:- H.Qrs.& 1 Coy. 1 Coy. 1 Coy.	LE TOURET. " " " "		GORRE CHATEAU. Take over Posts from Dehra Dun Bde. Handle of TUNING FORK.		
20th	58th Bde.	PARADIS area and VIEILLE CHAPELLE.		LOCON area.	Via LES LOBES.	Not to arrive in new area before 4-0 p.m.
20th	Divnl.Squadron.	LE QUENTIN.		LA PANNERIE.		

Date	Unit	From Area	Time	To Destination	Route	Remarks
October Night 20th/21st	1 Bn. 57th Bde.	Trenches CADBURY to VINE STREET		Intermediate line by ESTAMINET CORNER.	RUE LE L'EPINETTE	In support of new Ind I. Relieved by Garhwal Bde.
	1 Bn. 57th Bde.	Trenches		LACOUTURE (exclusive of farm at X 5 c 8.8.)		In support of new Ind III Bde. for the night.
	2 Bns. 57th Bde.	Bde. Reserve.		Trenches from THE LOOP (exclusive) to ORKNEY Road (inclusive)		Relieving a portion of Dehra Lun Bde. Times etc. to be arranged between Bdes.
	H.Qrs. 67th Bde.	Present billets.	On completion of relief.	LOISNE CHATEAU.		
21st	H.Qrs. 15th Divn.	FOSSE		LOCON		
	Divl. Cyclist Coy. Divl. Sig. Sec. Divl. Mob. Vet. Sec.	FOSSE. " "		W 11 b 2.8. Factory, LOCON. LOCON.		
21st	1 Bn. 57th Bde.	LACOUTURE		LE HAMEL.	Via LE TOURET.	Time to be arranged with Dehra Lun Bde.

N.B. The Battalion of 57th Brigade now garrisoning Posts and Keeps will be relieved as regards these garrisons by a Company from the Garhwal Brigade during afternoon of 20th instant. Orders as to Divl. Train and Field Ambulances will be issued later.

Addendum to 19th Division Order No. 15.
****

22nd October 1915.

1. The subdivision of the Divisional front into Sections will be readjusted; the point of division between Ind I and Ind II will be the intersection of BOMB LANE with the front line, S 27 a 9½.1., inclusive to Ind II.
    PIONEER ROAD will be common to both Sections.

2. This readjustment will take place tomorrow, 23rd inst., under arrangements to be made between Brigadiers.

3. The position of points of division between subsections, if altered by this rearrangement, will be reported to Divl. H.Q. as soon as fixed.

                                                    Lieutenant-Colonel.
                                                    General Staff.

Copies to:-
    File
    War Diary
    G.O.C.
    G.S.
    A.A.&.Q.M.G.
    G.O.C.,R.A.
    C.R.E.
    56th Infantry Brigade.
    57th   ,,   ,,
    58th   ,,   ,,

    O.C. 5th S.Wales Borderers.
    Divl.Train.
    M.M.G.Battery.
    A.D.M.S.
    Indian Corps.
    Divl.Signal Coy.
    Divl.Cavalry.
    Divl.Cyclists.

19th Division Order No. 15.

22nd October 1915.

1. 58th Brigade will relieve 56th Brigade in Ind II on the night of 24th/25th inst. All details of relief to be arranged between Brigadiers.

2. Garrisons of posts may be relieved during the day; otherwise no movement east of RUE DE L'EPINETTE before 5-45 p.m.

3. G.O.C. 58th Brigade will assume command of Ind II on completion of the relief.

4. Progress of the relief to be reported to Divl. H.Q.

Issued at 2-30 p.m.

Lieutenant-Colonel,
General Staff.

Copies to :-
File.
War Diary.
G.O.C.
G.S.
A.A.&.Q.M.G.
G.O.C.,R.A.
C.R.E.
56th Infy.Bde.
57th   "   "
58th   "   "

5/S.W.Borderers.
Divnl. Train.
M.M.Gun Battery.
A.D.M.S.
Indian Corps.
Meerut Division.
Divnl. Signal Coy.
    "   Cavalry.
    "   Cyclists.

SECRET.   19th Division No.G.A.692.

[Stamp: ORDERLY ROOM 27 OCT. 1915]

    The subjoined memo by G.O.C. 57th Brigade refers primarily to the defence of IND.IV, but there is much in it of general interest. The Major-General agrees with the principles enunciated, and desires officers to give them careful consideration.

H.Q.19th Division,   Lieut-Colonel,
15th October 1915.   General Staff.

ARGUMENTS IN FAVOUR OF COUNTER-ATTACKING ACROSS THE OPEN.

    An advance by communication trenches is the only other method, which is open to the following grave disadvantages :-

a. The communication trenches are very narrow and in wet weather very difficult to move in, except at a slow pace. There are not sufficient trenches to get a large body of men forward quickly, even if the present ones were dry and in thorough repair. This especially applies to IND.IV.a. Lately after a short spell of rain, it was found impossible to use any communication trenches in this subsection for relieving purposes.

b. Experience has shown us that the enemy have the range and direction of our communication trenches. Therefore there is no doubt but that they would shell them heavily during the attack and after the front line trench had been taken.

c. The difficulty of commanding a long line of men running up communication trenches continually under shell fire is prohibitive.

d. The communication trench might be held by an enemy's bombing party and even if this was successfully engaged by our own Grenadiers, the delay would probably be fatal even though our men immediately left the trench and advanced over the open.

e. When communication trenches are long and difficult a large number of men would lose their dash and others would lose themselves. It is doubtful if there would be any cohesion in the counter-attack.

    Owing to the above disadvantages, I strongly advise counter-attacking over the open by successive lines of men at six paces interval and a distance of 40 - 50 yards. The advance should be conducted by rapid rushes of 50 yards taking advantage of all cover, which can be ascertained by careful reconnaissance and shown the men who will take part in the attack. Some means of getting the extended lines out in front of Reserve trench parapet otherwise than clambering over the parapet should be devised. It is suggested that openings might be made at points in the communication trench where crouching men would be covered from view and they could dash out and lie down preparatory to the advance.

    During the advance and while preparatory movements are being made, the artillery should be requested to vigorously shell the enemy's parapets and special points where it has previously been ascertained that machine gun emplacements are. These must especially be looked for behind the enemy's front line on commanding ground or in ruined houses. It will be from these we shall suffer must. Any of the enemy's machine guns which accompany his attack will have to be put in exposed positions, possibly on our front line or support parapet and must be dealt with by the keeps and guns which accompany the flanking parties. A portion of the artillery could also be turned on to our front line trenches, but great care will have to be taken to signal back when our men are nearing the occupied trenches. The use of artillery in the counter-attack should be earnestly discussed between battalion and battery commanders for on their co-operation will depend the possibility of making what is really a frontal attack in the open.

All ground between the present local reserve trenches and the support line i.e., where the enemy's artillery can shell, must be passed as rapidly as possible. The nearer our troops get to the front lines, the freer they will be from artillery fire, therefore commanding officers must make sure that the ground over which the men will work, is free of wire or any other obstacle.

Crowding must be carefully guarded against and every care taken not to give the enemy an easy stationary target.

There is a distinct probability that the enemy's artillery will be lifted, immediately the front trench is occupied, on to the old British trench and the RUE DU BOIS.

This being the case, the local reserves should be organized and advanced as rapidly as possible in order to anticipate it. The rapidity with which the counter attack takes place is the essence of the whole and on it will depend the success and the number of casualties. Every man _must_ know his place, his line of advance and objective. Bombing parties must shove ahead, without hesitation, and be backed up by a continual stream of carriers.

These carriers must, if possible, be able to throw bombs.

There will be considerable difficulty in getting the Brigade Reserve battalion across the RUE DU BOIS to the old British trench on account of the enemy's barrage. The Officer Commanding the reserve battalion will therefore carefully reconnoitre the approaches from the Brigade Reserve assembly posts adjacent to EDWARD and ALBERT roads and note those which afford the best cover. Each platoon must know line of advance from the assembly trench to its objective or point of attack in the front line. The flanking half companies must be told off at once, explained their duty and ordered to reconnoitre their ground.

Finally the G.O.C. wishes to impress on all Regimental officers the importance of getting together as many company bombers as possible, giving them much practice with live bombs and continual throwing exercises with dummies. Battalions can greatly assist during the time they are in rest billets.

Live bombs can always be drawn from the Grenadier School. Bombing parties must always be properly organized with a view of keeping up a good supply during an engagement.

=== ******* ===

NOT TO BE TAKEN FURTHER FORWARD THAN SUBSECTION H.Q.

"A" Form. Army Form C. 2121.
MESSAGES AND SIGNALS.

| Prefix | Code | m. | Words | Charge | This message is on a/c of | Rec'd. at | m. |

Secret Priority

Sent At / To / By

ORDERLY ROOM 31 OCT 1915 19TH DIV CYCLIST CO

TO: OC Div Squadron 19" Cyclists Salvage Company

Sender's Number: A/137
Day of Month: 31/10
AAA

Cancel my Secret instructions no Q/92/Z & No 94/3 everything postponed aaa Return my No Q/92 Z Secret instructions.

From: 19th Division
Place:
Time: 10-15 am

(Z) M Davies Lt Col

SECRET.  1st Army, General Staff,
No.G.S.61. Dated 26/10/15.

Adv. 1st Army.

Reference O.A.775 of 22nd March 1915, reissued with O.A.845 of 13th September, and amended by O.A.63 of 12th October, the following supplementary orders are issued as regards firing on airships.

1. **By night.**
Except over certain proscribed areas known by the French as "Zones de Sécurité" all airships will be regarded as hostile unless they make the special signal laid down in the letter referred to above. This signal is intended as a warning against fire from our own troops in the event of an airship finding it necessary to fly over ground outside the limits of a "Zone de Sécurité" and as an additional guarantee when flying over a "Zone de Sécurité".

2. **By Day.**
Airships will be fired on as soon as their hostile identity has been established. To assist in the identification the French authorities have been asked to provide diagrams showing the different types of airships in use by the French Army. Copies will be issued to all concerned when received. The presumption, however, will always be that an airship outside a "Zone de Sécurité" is hostile.

3. The only "Zone de Sécurité" in the British Area is that portion of the Third Army Area West of the AMIENS – DOULLENS road. This zone extends westwards to the sea coast.

(Sgd) E.L.Tandy, Lt.Col.
for Lieut. General,
Chief of the General Staff.

G.H.Q.
24th October 1915.

19th Division No. I.881.

TO :-   Headquarters,
53th, 57th, 58th Inf.Bdes.
R.A., R.E., 5/S.W.E.
M.M.Gun Bty, Cyclist Coy,
Yorkshire Dragoons.

Copy of above is forwarded for information with reference to my I.758 dated 14/10/15.

Major,
General Staff.

H.Q.19th Division,
29th October 1915.

R

Secret

Defence Scheme
19th Division, Indian Corps.

October 1915

Reference to (a) 1/40,000 combined sheet. BETHUNE
(b) Corps Trench Map.

1. General Organization

The Division is organized for the defence of its front as follows:-
(a) Two Brigades in front line, each of which has two battalions in front line and two in Brigade Reserve.
(b) One Brigade in Divisional Reserve.

2. Frontages

(a) The present Divisional front extends from GRENADIER ROAD (inclusive) — A3 c 1.2. to PIPE communication trench (inclusive). It is divided into two sections (Brigade fronts) known as IND I and IND II; the 1st Corps holds the front on our right, and the Meerut Division holds IND III and IND IV on our left.

The point of division between IND I and IND II is the junction of BOMB LANE (3.27) a 9k.1.) with the front line, inclusive to IND II.

(c) Each of the sections is divided into two sub-sections (battalion fronts) as follows:-

IND.I.A. From the right of Divisional front to A.3.a.2.8%.
Frontage ... 850 yds.

IND.I.B. Thence to BOMB LANE, 3.27 a 9k.1. (inclusive)
Frontage ... 800 yds.

IND.II.A. BOMB LANE (exclusive) to junction of road east of ORCHARD SUPPORT trench with front line (inclusive)
Frontage ... 900 yds.

IND.II.B. Thence to left of Divisional front
Frontage ... 750 yds.

Note: PIONEER ROAD in common to both sections.

3. Boundaries

(a) (i) On the south the Divisional area is bounded as follows:-
GRENADIER ROAD — LE PLANTIN SOUTH — south arm of TUNING FORK — BORRE WOOD (all inclusive) — south arm of D'ESSARS — LONG CORNET — AVELETTE (all inclusive) — ECLUSE along the LA-BASSÉE — AIRE canal to DOUCE CRÈME Fe.

(ii) On the west boundary is:-
DOUCE CRÈME Fe. — MANOVOIS (exclusive) — CARVIN — LES RUES DES VACHES (both inclusive).

(iii) On the north boundary is:-
PIPE communication trench — DEAD COW front — HAYSTACK front (both inclusive) — CHAVATTES front (inclusive) — LE TOURET NORTH fort (inclusive) — PASSLE — LES LOBES — BOHEME (all inclusive) — QUENTIN (exclusive) — LES RUES DES VACHES. (vide also Appendix I)

4. System of Defence

The following system of defence organization is in the Divisional Area in Front system is adhered to

(A) Front system includes:-

(1) Front trenches. A continuous firing line, partly revetted, fairly broad wire.

Support trenches — these, when completed, are intended to form a second continuous firing line about 90 yards in rear of the front trenches, provided with dugouts to hold from 60% to 80% of the front line garrison under normal conditions and also to form shelter to the additional men who will be hurriedly drawn from the front trenches in the event of a serious bombardment or communication trenches will be provided to connect the two lines with the front line and the support.

(2) Keeps. Two of the points to be held as the outputs trenches is a line of keeps which are intended to break up an attack, which has penetrated the front support line, and to give time to the organization of counter-attacks from the keeps, stocked with rations and water for 3 days ammunition for rifle, 1800 rounds per machine gun; they are to front line keeps garrison or maximum garrisons.

(x) Calculated on maximum garrisons.

(x) for this see "Keeps" given in APPENDIX I.

and are provided with obligatory garrisons as there shown. These garrisons are not available for defensive action. They are never to be allowed to fall below the strength laid down.

(4) <u>Reserve Trenches</u>. In the rear of the first line of keeps, and connected to the support line by communication trenches which at present are about 300 yards apart on the average, are the reserve trenches. These are chiefly breastworks and form a second, and in some parts of the front a third line of resistance. They are provided with a certain amount of shelter for local reserves.

(5) <u>Supporting Points</u>. In the front system there are certain fortified posts in the neighbourhood of the Reserve Trenches, which are intended to fulfil the same tactical purposes as the forward keeps in the event of a hostile attack penetrating our lines still further.

These posts (which are enumerated in Appendix I, "2nd line Keeps" and "3rd line Keeps") will be stocked with 100 rounds reserve ammunition per rifle,ᵟ 10,000 rounds per machine gunᵟ, preserved rations ᵟ and water for one day and 100 bombs each. They will be provided with obligatory garrisons, detailed from Brigades in front line, as shown in Appendix 3. Their garrisons are available for offensive action if situation demands it. Normally a portion of the Brigade reserves will also be in occupation of some of these posts.

B. CROIX BARBÉE ~~System~~

This forms part of a defended belt of country extending from GRENAY (7½ miles S.E. of BETHUNE) to FLEURBAIX (3 miles S.W. of ARMENTIERES.) In and near the Divisional area its front line is roughly LE PLANTIN --- FESTUBERT -- RICHEBOURG ST. VAAST, its rear line GORRÉ -- LE TOURET --- LACOUTURE.

(a) It consists of:
~~Along~~ its front a line of defended localities and posts ~~known~~ as ~~the~~ "Village" Line; in the Divisional area this includes the two hamlets of LE PLANTIN, --- ~~FESTUBERT~~ -- & the village of FESTUBERT, and the straggling street called the RUE DE L'EPINETTE.

ᵟ Calculated on obligatory garrisons. Should the obligatory garrisons be reinforced in view of an ~~impending~~ hostile attack an extra equivalent of reserve ammunition, etc. will be stocked at the line under Divisional arrangements.

In the CROIX BARBEE System the posts and defended localities of this forward line alone have obligatory garrisons and stocks of reserve ammunition and rations* (detailed in Appendix I). If conditions are such as to command offensive action by the Divisional reserves, these garrisons will be available to join their brigades.

(v) Continuous lines of breastwork ---
    (I) The "Intermediate" or "Tuning Fork" line running from the LA BASSEE Canal through A.8.c. to X.29.a.
    II The "Le Touret" line running from the canal through F.5.a. to LE TOURET, thence along the RUE DES CHAVATTES towards COUR ST VAAST.

(c) Other fortified posts in the neighbourhood of the continuous lines; these are not stocked with reserves of ammunition and rations, and are only provided with caretaking guards (See Appendix I)

The object of these posts, in the neighbourhood and other defences is, like the keeps in the front system, to break up and hold a hostile attack, should it penetrate so far through our line, pending the organization of counter-attacks.

(C) ESSARS --- BOUT DEVILLE System.

The general system of defence is completed by this third defended belt, in rear of the CROIX BARBEE system, which also contains a number of detached fortified posts (see Appendix I) With the exception of LE HAMEL post, which is guarded by the Brigade Reserve battalion at present billeted in LE HAMEL, caretaking guards for these posts are furnished by the Brigade in Divisional Reserve.

5. Distribution of Troops

(A) Infantry. The infantry are disposed in trenches & billets as follows:-

IND.I. One Infantry Brigade

    H.Q. LOISNE

    I. ~~Front line~~ Two battalions in subsections IND.I.A. and IND.I.B.

        IND.I.A. H.Q - intersection of FIFE ROAD with the old British Trench --- A.2.c.10.6 at present; normally 3 companies in firing line and support, 1 company in local reserve. Machine Guns in firing line 3
        local reserves in GROUSE BUTTS, etc
        Communications -- up FIFE ROAD; down STUART ROAD.

---

* Calculated on obligatory garrisons. Should the obligatory garrisons be reinforced in view of an impending hostile attack, an extra equivalent of reserve ammunition etc, will be stocked at the time under Divisional arrangements.

IND I.B. H.Q., just north of intersection of QUINQUE-RUE and Old British Trench ... S 26 a 2.9.
At present normally 2 companies in firing line and support, 2 companies in local reserve.
Machine guns in firing line 6
  "   "   " local reserve   1
Local Reserves in reserve line trenches
Communications up BARNTON and PIONEER ROADS
                down, LOTHIAN ROAD.

Note. When dugouts have been fully provided in support trenches, the proportion of the troops in the trenches is to be :-
  in firing line 25%
  in support 25%
  in local reserve 50%

II Brigade Reserves
  (a) 1 Battalion -- H.Q., just north of the intersection of Old British Trench with WILLOW ROAD;
       1 Company occupying LE PLANTIN. E., FESTUBERT E. LE PLANTIN S., LE PLANTIN. N. FESTUBERT.
       3 Companies in Old British Trench.
  (b) 1 Battalion -- at present at LE HAMEL; will be moved up to Intermediate line when accommodation has been improved. Moves there at once in case of alarm.

IND. II. One Infantry Brigade
  H.Q. CSE. DU RAUX.

  I Front line Two battalions in subsections IND II A and IND II. B.

  IND II A H.Q., in Old English Trench near INDIAN VILLAGE ... S 20 v 6.1.
           At present, normally 3 companies in firing line & support, 1 in local reserve
           Machine Guns in firing line 2
             "   "   " support   2
           local reserve in old British Trench - will be moved forward into RICHMOND TRENCH as soon as the trench is completed
           Communications -- up PIONEER ROAD and SHETLAND ROAD; down ARGYLE ROAD.

  IND II.B. H.Q., in old British Trench near TUBE STATION ... S 21. a. 3.7
           At present, normally 3 companies in firing line and support, 1 in local reserve.
           Machine Guns in firing line 5
           local reserve in old British Trench.
           Communications ... up, ROPE Communication trench
                                  PIPE   "   "
                             down FUNNEL "   "

Note. When dugouts have been fully provided in support trenches, the proportion of troops in trenches is to be :-
  in firing line 25%
  in support 25%
  in local reserve 50%

II. **Brigade Reserves** At present disposed as follows:—

(a) 1 Battalion — H.Q. S.2.J.b.9.9.
  In posts & houses on the line CAILLOUX
  posts --- RUE DE L'EPPINETTE ---
  CHAVATTES post.

(b) 1 Battalion — H.Q. S.16.b.1.8.
  About LE TOURET.

In case of alarm (a) moves at once to old British Trench; (b) forms up in X.17.a and C. with its right on the CSE. DU RAUX, ready to move to RUE DE L'EPINETTE by the RUE DU BOIS and Routes B. & C.

As soon as RICHMOND TRENCH is completed, (a) will be accommodated in the Old British Trench, and (b) in the RUE DE L'EPINETTE line.

(E) **Divisional Mounted Troops.**

The Divisional Cavalry are billeted in W.10.b. and the Cyclist Coy in W.11.a. Under normal conditions they are employed chiefly in defence work, including especially the important duty of improvement of the drainage system. A detachment of the Cyclists is at D.H.Q and another is employed on Salvage work.

(F) **M.M.G. Battery.**

Employed by sections in rear of the front system in positions from which their indirect long range fire can be used with effect.

(G) **Medical Arrangements**

AID. POSTS. IND I. A .... A.2. central
             B A.26.d.11
             IND II. A .... S.20.d.5.3.
             B   .... S.21.a.3.7.

Advanced Dressing Stations

IND. I.   MARAIS - F.5.b.0.3
IND II   RUE-DU-BOIS - X.17.a.5.5.

Field Ambulances. (1) MESPLAUX - X.14.a.10.7.
                  (2) LOCON —
                  (3) BOIS DE PACAUT - Q.23.b.7.6.

6. **Principles of Defence**

(1) The broad principles of defence in the event of a hostile attack, or of the line being penetrated at any point; will be as follows:—

(a) Troops will not fall back from any one line to any other line, but all points will be defended whether their flanks are turned or not.

(b) Should the enemy succeed in penetrating our defences, keeps previously garrisoned, together with communication trenches prepared for fire both ways, will hold him up in a pocket in which his flanks will be exposed to our fire, to attack by bombs and to counter attack.

(c) All subordinate commanders must realize that no ground which might be held should be given up. The objective of every leader should be to deliver a counter attack as rapidly as possible. With this objective in view subordinate commanders should usually reinforce their support lines so as to have sufficient troops immediately at hand so as to make a local counter attack. Unless this is done, time will be lost, and the opportunity for delivering an immediate counter attack gone.

(d) Troops designated for counter attack should be fresh and located where they are protected from artillery fire, protection being specially constructed for this purpose where necessary.

(ii) To minimise losses and obtain shelter it is necessary to dispose troops holding the trenches in considerable depth. In case of hostile attack, therefore, the question of communications becomes of paramount importance, whether for reinforcements of forward lines or for the organization of counter attacks. All officers must therefore study the communications in their area; Commanders of all grades, each in his own sphere, must think of possible contingencies and have plans of action ready prepared to meet them. Brigade Commanders have prepared their local schemes of defence, and will see that their subordinate commanders do the same for their respective commands.

(iii) The firing line is to be considered as the line of resistance, and will be held at all costs. At the same time, unless the firing line be slightly held during a hostile bombardment preliminary to an attack, unnecessary losses will be incurred. To permit the holding of the line on this system, however, ample communication trenches are required between the firing line and support trenches and the latter must be provided with accommodation (as nearly bomb proof as possible) and not only for its own garrison but for most of the garrison of the firing line as well. For the same reason support trenches must be near enough to the firing line to allow troops who have sheltered in them during a bombardment to get back to the firing line when the bombardment ceases, before the attacking enemy can reach it. At the same time the support trenches should be at such a distance from the firing line that the bombardment of the support trench will have to be a separate operation from the bombardment of the firing line.

(IV) An immediate counter attack, such as should be delivered by local reserves, is more likely to be successful, even though in no great strength, than a more deliberate & stronger counter attack delivered after the enemy has had time to consolidate his gains.

It may prove to be preferable to send counter attack across the open, rather than up communication trenches, when the latter are being swept by hostile artillery, or when they are likely to be too congested for rapid advance.

V. A most important part of any counter attack is the prompt organization of bombing attacks from the flanks up the captured trenches. Parties of trained grenadiers must therefore be kept stationed for this purpose in support and reserve trenches, ready in case of attack to move at once when required, and initiate bombing counter attacks. Each of these parties must be organized to include bomb-throwers, bomb carriers with sandbags, and bayonet men. The supply of bombs to these parties is most important, and maps will be prepared showing the positions of all bomb stores. Their positions must be known to those who will use them, and they must be clearly marked by signboards, etc. The normal supply for a subsection will be.

300 bombs in front line
500 Bombs in support line
1200 Bombs in reserve line.

These are replenished from Brigade reserve of bombs and these again from Divisional Reserve.

VI. At all times it is essential to maintain the offensive spirit, and to gain and keep superiority over the enemy in all points, bombing, sniping, patrolling. Any damage or loss he may inflict must be repaired at once with heavy interest.

7. Action in case of attack

A. Alarm Signals. The following will be used as alarm signals.

(1) "Enemy's Infantry attacking" – GREEN rocket followed immediately by a white rocket – repeated every 30 seconds interval.

(2) "Heavy artillery or trench mortar bombardment of our trenches" GREEN rocket followed immediately by RED & repeated as above.

(3) "Our own shells falling short – lengthen range" TWO RED rockets sent up and repeated in a similar manner to signal (1) & (2).

Parachute asteroid rockets will be used. These signals are supplementary to other means of communication, such as telephones, and not in substitution for them.

B. **Action by troops not in trenches**

(1) Working parties of Engineers will return immediately to their billets, where units will remain in readiness to move as required.

(2) Battalions in Brigade Reserve will move under the orders of G.O.C. Brigades in front line – see 5 (A) above.

(3) The Brigade in Divisional Reserve (which must be held ready to move at 1½ hours' notice) will move as follows:

(a) Should the enemy attack or penetrate the defences IND I, it will assemble west of GORRE, forming up from F.3.a and b. Telegraphic order – "Concentrate GORRE"

Routes

(i) Battalions S of LOCON crossroads, via trestle bridge at X 13 d 7.9., along canal bank to X 13.d.4.1. – X 20 c 5. 3. – X 20. c. 3.3 track (not marked on map) through X 26 central to F. 3. a. 0. 9.

(ii) Battalions north of LOCON crossroads, and Brigade H.Q., via both PONT TOURNANT and trestle bridge at X.8.b. 1.1. – MESPLAUX – X 21 central – road junction X 27.c.

(b) Should the enemy attack or penetrate the defences in IND.II., the Brigade in Divisional Reserve will assemble west of LE TOURET, forming up about X 16 a and c. Telegraphic order – "Concentrate LE TOURET"

Routes

(i) Brigade H.Q. and Battalions south of LOCON cross roads, via both PONT TOURNANT and trestle bridge X 13 d 7.9. – crossroads X 21 a. 9. 9.

(ii) Battalions north of LOCON cross roads, by trestle bridges at X 8.b. 1.1. and X.3.a. 3.5. – X 8.b.9.2. – X 15 b 2. 8.

Each Brigade going into reserve for the first time will send out officers to reconnoitre the above routes and forming up places as soon as possible after it goes into reserve.

In the event of a serious attack it may be necessary to order a portion of the Reserve Brigade to occupy the post and defended localities in the CROIX BARBEE system. The Reserve Brigade will therefore be prepared to do so at short notice; troops will detailed for the purpose, and the necessary reconnaissances of posts and routes will be carried out

(4) The Divisional Cavalry and Cyclists, if in billets, will assemble about W.6.d. central and the senior officer will get into communication with Divisional H.Q. by the telephone which will be left at H.Q. Reserve Brigade at that place.

If at work in the forward area, Divisional Mounted troops will form up and proceed to the vicinity of Advanced Divisional Headquarters at LOISNE

(5) 5/S.W. Borderers will form up at alarm posts, in Divisional Reserve. In the event of the enemy attacking or penetrating the defences of IND I, the detachment at LE TOURET will be called to Battalion H.Q at BORRE.

8. **Report Centres.**

In the event of a serious hostile attack, advanced Report Centres will be established as follows:-

Indian Corps.   LESTREM. (BETHUNE)
Left Division, 1st Corps.   White house VIELLE CHAPELLE
~~Meerut Division~~
19th Division   LOISNE.
   IND. I   Wylch chapel, A.1.d.6.9.
   IND. II   RUE DE CAILLOUX S.20.e.5.2.

sgd. A.E. Buckle
Lieut. Col.
General Staff.

H.Q. 19th Division
31st October 1915

Appendix II
Instructions Regarding Posts

The following instructions will be observed regarding posts whether in front or CROIX BARBEE Systems:—

I. All stores will be kept in boarded recesses, closed by doors. Doors are to be clearly marked with the designation of the stores to be found inside. Bombs will be stored separate from other articles.

II. An accurate list of stores on charge will be kept at each post and will be produced for inspection when required.

III. The Brigadier Commanding the section will arrange for the periodical turnover of the stores on charge. The water would be renewed at least once every two days.

IV. The obligatory garrison of each post will be utilized for keeping the post in proper repair and in carrying out any improvement required. Where posts are being reconstructed or strengthened the garrison is responsible that all work finished is kept clean and in proper repair. The garrison will also be at the disposal of the R.E. in charge of the reconstruction for work on improvement being carried out.

V. The obligatory garrison of the post may be used for other work outside in the vicinity of the post. The G.O.C. Section must however use his discretion as to the number of men who can be withdrawn for work at any time from any particular post. At least one quarter of the obligatory garrison must always remain on duty in each post.

VI. The Commander of any keep or post must understand that, in case of hostile attack, it will be his duty to hold out at all costs. This must be constantly borne in mind in thinking out what improvements are required.

VII. The Commander of the obligatory garrison of a post is responsible:—
   (a) That when taking over a post he checks the stores and reports any deficiency, and any defect in the post itself to superior authority.

(b) That the post is maintained in a proper state of repair and sanitation.

(c) That all military precautions are observed

(d) That on relief he hands over the post and its stores correct to the incoming garrison, together with any useful information as regard its defence.

(e) That a range card for the post is kept up-to-date and handed over on relief to the Commander of the incoming garrison.

Ig. F. Sisili. Cycl. Cry:
Vol: 4

131/7694

Nov 15.

Army Form C. 2118

WAR DIARY
INTELLIGENCE SUMMARY
(Erase heading not required.)

19th Division Cyclist Coy

1st November to 30th November 1915

Volume IV

Rudolf Smith Capt.
O.C. 19th DIV. CYCLIST CO.

Army Form C. 2118

Sheet No 14

WAR DIARY
or
INTELLIGENCE SUMMARY
(Erase heading not required.)

Place	Date	Hour	Summary of Events and Information	Remarks and references to Appendices
HINGETTE	1/11/15		Unsettled weather. Coy. have baths in LOCON, commencing at 9.30 am. Cycle to "Forward Area" to continue digging operations. Condition at 12.30 pm renders continuation of work impossible. Men NCOs go on leave by 4.05 am train from CALONNE.	5am
	2/11/15		Continued very wet. Had NCO. boats in an almost impassable condition. The Coy. "Stood by" as cycling was nearly an impossibility.	5am
	3/11/15		Unsettled weather. Work continued in "Forward Area". The finished parts of the new duty holding up to 10" of water. Men have to work in gum boots & waders.	5am
	4/11/15		Dull – no rain. Work progressing slowly owing to heavy state of ground & generally of roads. The "water level" appears the within 6 or 9 ins surface at the bank. Work continued in continued has nearly ordinary. NCO. Warren detailed by C.R.E. am. 3 NCOs to men detailed R.O.C. Trench Tramway STANTST POST. (M32a Map 36 Corps Sheet BETHUNE) bringing substances a substantial revetment had the controls in the ditch close to its approach to the RUE DU BOIS, and another near the orchard.	5am
	5/11/15		Dull – work continued. 19th Division order No 76 states that GOC XI th CORPS takes over line now held by INDIAN CORPS at 10 am Nov 10. N.F. CORPS to consist of 7 GUARDS, 19 & 8 46th Divisions. R. Air. takes over front now held by LAHORE and MEERUT Div? on night 10/11th Nov. The	

1875 Wt. W593/826 1,000,000 4/15 J.B.C. & A. A.D.S.S./Forms/C. 2118.

Army Form C. 2118

WAR DIARY
or
INTELLIGENCE SUMMARY
(Erase heading not required.)

Sheet 15.

Place	Date	Hour	Summary of Events and Information	Remarks and references to Appendices
HINGETTE	6/11/15		The Guards Div. relieve 20th Div. on night of 7/8th from DUCK'S BILL (M.35/10.0 Sheet 36a) inclusive to FAUQUISSART ROAD inclusive. The 4th Bn. is per S.W. on per 1st Street (inclusive). A new lane the details to report to O.C. Sigs also 19th Bn. LOCON on the 7th inst.	Jam
	7/11/15		Fine, clear cold. Stable at 9.30 am. Capt. C. Herbert Smith goes on leave, also 1 N.C.O. It is interesting at this stage, to compute the actual strength of the Coy in Coy Billets. The Actual Strength (not Establishment) is 204 plus 2 A.S.C drivers. 117 men are detached and 9 are resting & complete. This leaves us with 80 (not army 2 ASC). It must be remembered that of this number several are necessarily employed, i.e. Cooks, pioneers, orderlies, batmen etc. The attached appendix Shows detail.	See Appendix IV jam
	8/11/15		Clear, not continued. 1 O.C. 19th D.C.C from 19 Div. H.Q. "arrange to move two billets in "farm at X8L.83." (Sheet 36a) on 9th inst are Q.M. Stores billets are required for Supply sections of Trains in which runs two farm ward addresses & which repeatedly "19th Divisional Train." Billets fixed up as ordered.	Jam
LE CASAN	9/11/15		Mostly dull. Coy moved into billet near LE CASAN X86.83 (Sheet 36a) at 11 am. Orderly Room at X8L.46. On arrival several fatigue parties were at once put to work to clean & tidy the billets etc. This place had been left in an appalling filthy condition much to the resentment of the occupiers. 2 NCO's go on leave.	Jam

1875 Wt. W593/826 1,000,000 4/15 J.B.C. & A. A.D.S.S./Forms/C. 2118.

WAR DIARY or INTELLIGENCE SUMMARY

Army Form C. 2118

Sheet 16.

Place	Date	Hour	Summary of Events and Information	Remarks and references to Appendices
LE CASAN (LOOSN)	10/11/15		Very windy. Wind Suly S. Work continued — heavy rain & wind like a gale. Work stopped at 12.30 owing to impossible conditions.	
	11/11/15		Very fine, cold. S. wind. Work continued — the sides of the ditch had slipped in many places. Fort at end of day the ditch was almost finished. XI Corps Routine Orders now issued by Major General F.R. BARR of CAVAN C.B., M.O., Commanding.	
	12/11/15		Very wet indeed. Wind in the S. Men on A.P.M. Control Post reliefs. One man gone on leave 9 pm.	
	13/11/15		Wind almost due W. blowing half a gale with a heavy driving rain. Conditions gent. impossible for work. Ptes 5090 Newton W.F. & 6047 Bailey W.H. evacuated from Amb. Area Station. 9 am not respectively. Pte 5090 Newton W.F. strgm. as reinforcement. 2nd H.A.K. R.C. 10 A.C.C. following reinforcement arrive ALBANS 220 hours. Lydiate Cpl Sinew "Boydon and Please enough to meet". L6555 Pte Clara who went sick 2 days ago has a slight attack of "Trench feet". This may be result of mottans naked in the RIVER LOTSME in September last. Point in my OPIE it is exceptional. At the time of wear & tegg weather conditions which have been trying no means extreme.	
	14/11/15		Healthy, Calm & Shown. Cpls Pte O'Ley, 11 evacuated to KIMERVILLE. 3344 Left thinks W. 3867 Pte Smith T., 4736 Pte Pierce J., 6693 McCarrick J., 7795 Pte Parker M. join as reinforcements from 101 Infantry Base Depot Review. Inspection by Co. There was a voluntary service for Roman Catholics at LOOSN. Leave all cancelled owing to closure of Port of BOULOGNE.	

Army Form C. 2118

WAR DIARY
or
INTELLIGENCE SUMMARY
(Erase heading not required.)

Sheet 17.

Place	Date	Hour	Summary of Events and Information	Remarks and references to Appendices
LE CASAN (LOCON)	18/11/15		Weather fine but very cold. Work continued in forward area. There was 216' of notes in the ditch & a few more cases of subsidence of the banks, causing much extra labour. Capt. C.H. SMITH not returned from leave - Boulogne still closed.	JPM
	19/11/15		Weather continues fine. Capt Charlot Smith returned from leave. The subsidence of the ditch were nearly all repaired.	JPM
	20/11/15		Weather shown very foggy + cold. Some rain. Ditch was opened for use. Continued repairs to sides of ditch which keep left well fit for use. 6073 Pte Oxley W returned (1) 17S Lt G. Allen Morris gone on leave.	JPM
	21/11/15			JPM
	22/11/15		Cpl. Share Father at Pont Riqueul. Sgt Livingston leave.	
	23/11/15		Fine Weather. Collected from work in ditch returned to R.E. Stores. Lieut E.O.H. Hassan returned from duty with 51st C.B. R.E. 217 C.M. Murray AVERLEY joined as reinforcement together with 241 Cpl. Edmonds Corp, 4264 Ptes Hiron T.T, 5702 Davis C., 5081 Daniel P., 6461 Brooksbank Co, from No.1 Inf. Base Depot.	JPM
	24/11/15		Reconnaissance for billets of St Floris by St Venant in division will move out 2 Sunday to XI Corps Reserve. Owing to much difficulty billets were taken over at St. Venant (Maps 36 & P.8 & 19) Sgt R.S. TALBOT returned to duty from 82 F.A. R.E.	JPM
ST. VENANT	25/11/15		Fine Roads in very bad condition. Coy moved into billets as allotted above. Billets clean of cycle clean H division. 10pm - 11pm so a chase. Roads in very bad condition. Continued frosts fog. Men returns from A.P.M. Post	JPM
	26/11/15			JPM

WAR DIARY

Sheet 18.

Place	Date	Hour	Summary of Events and Information	Remarks and references to Appendices
ST. VENANT	26/11/15		Rain had snow. Commencement of training while Division is in Reserve, starting with Platoon drill. The training will be progressive throughout the month the Division are not in the line.	
	27/11/15		Fine morning. Inspection of billets which are to be improved. Training continued. Some men returned from Trench Tramway duties.	
	28/11/15		Very hard frost. Training programme complied with next to ATK.R. for use later on. German aeroplane over billets. Returned fire — One brought down over LILLE. Voluntary service in R.C. Cy. Butts at LESTREM.	
	29/11/15		Atmospheric conditions in morning not suited, weather improvement continued. Football match arranged to keep up more interest & amusement and so on and other physical fitness.	
	30/11/15		Fine with a thaw set in. Training continued & much improvement in drill shown. Lecture given & route march in afternoon.	

Michael Smith CAPT.,
O.C. 19th DIV. CYCLIST CO.

Army Form C. 2118

WAR DIARY
or
INTELLIGENCE SUMMARY
(Erase heading not required.)

Appendix IV.

Place	Date	Hour	Summary of Events and Information	Remarks and references to Appendices

Details of detachments etc. from Coy.
Strength by G.M.M MORRIS; 2 Lieut, 19 Div. Cyclist Coy. 7/11/15

206 War Establishment (including 2 A.S.C. drivers).

36 NCOs & men attached 19 Div. H.Q.
9   1 Officer & 8 men attached 19 Div. Salvage Coy.
44 NCOs & men   "   duties under A.D.M.S. 19 Div. ⎫
2   1 Officer & 1 man "   81st Field Co. R.E.   ⎪
2   1   "   " 1 " "   82nd   "   "   ⎬ Attached
7   NCOs & men   "   C.R.E. 19th Div.   ⎪
4   men   "   19th Div. Signal Coy.   ⎪
13 NCOs & men   "   Trench Tramway Coys.   ⎭

117

1   Officer seconded 253rd Tunnelling Co. R.E. ⎫
1   2/Lieut having Complete Strength   ⎬ Having Complete
2   R.A.M.C. men   "   "   ⎪ Complete.
5   Privates   "   "   ⎭

9

126
80 Present with Coy. including 2 A.S.C. drivers
===

G.M.M.

SECRET.

Copy No. 23

19th DIVISION ORDER NO. 16.

6th November 1915.

Information. 1. The G.O.C., XIth Corps takes over the Command of the line now held by the Indian Corps at 10.0 a.m. on November 10th. The 19th Division will from that time be incorporated in the XIth Corps.
The 43th Division, XIth Corps, is taking over the front now held by Lahore and Meerut Divisions on the night of the 10th/11th November. The Guard's Division XIth Corps, on the night of 14th/15th November relieves the 20th Division from the DUCK'S BILL M.35.b.10.0 exclusive to FAUQUISSART Road exclusive and the 46th Division as far S.W. as 15th Street(inclusive).

Orders to Troops. 2. The 56th Brigade will relieve the 57th Brigade in Ind I on the night of the 9th/10th November. All details of relief to be arranged between Brigadiers.
Garrisons of Posts may be relieved during the day; otherwise no movement East of ESTAMINET CORNER will take place before 5-15 p.m.
The G.O.C., 56th Brigade will assume command of Ind I on completion of relief, which is to be reported to Divisional Headquarters.

Major, General Staff,
19th Division.

Issued at 11.30 a.m.

Copies to:-

File.   O.C.5th S.W.Borderers.
War Diary.   Divisional Train
G.O.C.   M.M.G.Battery.
G.S.   A.D.M.S.
A.A.& Q.M.G.   Indian Corps.
G.O.C., R.A.
C.R.E.   Divisional Signal Company.
56th Infantry Brigade.   Divisional Squadron.
57th   ,,   ,,   Divisional Cyclists.
58th   ,,   ,,

Divl. Cyclists.

[Stamp: ORDERLY ROOM, 15 NOV. 1915, 19TH DIV. CYCLIST Co.]

Copy No. 24

19th Division Order No. 17.
****

15th November 1915.

1. 57th Brigade will relieve 58th Brigade in the Left Section of the Divisional front on the night of 17th/18th November. Details will be arranged direct between Brigadiers concerned.

2. Garrisons of posts may be relieved during the day; no other movement of troops east of RUE DE L'EPINETTE will take place before 5.0 p.m.

3. G.O.C. 57th Brigade will assume command of the Section on completion of the relief, which will be reported to Divl. H.Q.

A. B. Buckle

Lieutenant-Colonel,
General Staff.

Issued at 10-30 a.m.

Copies to:-

File.
War Diary.
G.O.C.
G.S.
A.A.& Q.M.G.
G.O.C., R.A.
C.R.E.
56th Infantry Brigade.
57th   ,,   ,,
58th   ,,   ,,

O.C. 5th S.Wales Borderers.
Divisional Train.
M.M.G. Battery.
A.D.M.S.
XIth Corps.
7th Division.
Divl. Signal Company.
Divl. Squadron.
Divl. Cyclists.

****

Copy No. 36

19th Division Order No. 18.
****

19th November 1915.

References to 1/40,000 Maps 36 A and BETHUNE Combined Sheet, and Trench Map.

INFORMATION	1.	The frontages of Corps in the First Army will be readjusted. When the readjustment is complete the front of the XIth Corps will extend from the intersection of LA QUINQUE RUE with front line (exclusive) to the vicinity of PICANTIN. It will be held by 46th Division on the right and Guards Division on the left, with the 19th Division in Army Reserve.

The left of the Ist Corps front is to be held by 7th Division.

KINKROO communication trench is allotted to 46th Division; KINKROO Keep, INDIAN VILLAGE tramway, and LE TOURET EAST and CENTRAL Posts to 7th Division.

The R.E. Depot and the bomb store at X 15 d 9.3. remains in the hands of the right division of the XIth Corps.

INFANTRY RELIEFS
56th Bde.
2. (a) On night of 23rd/24th November 56th Bde. will hand over the portion of its front from the right as far as A 3 a 3.0. to 21st Bde. of 7th Divn., and the remainder of its front to 20th Bde. of 7th Divn.

57th Bde.
(b) On night of 24th/25th November 57th Bde. will hand over from its present right to the intersection of LA QUINQUE RUE with front line (inclusive) to 20th Bde. of 7th Divn., and the remainder of its front to 46th Divn.

Details of the above reliefs will be arranged by Brigadiers with the commanders of the Brigades of 7th and 46th Divisions concerned.

Brigadiers will hand over the command of their respective fronts on completion of reliefs.

Posts will be handed over to 7th and 46th Divns. in accordance with Appendix I, under Brigade arrangements.

ARTILLERY RELIEFS
3. The Divl. Artillery will be relieved as follows on the nights of 21st/22nd and 22nd/23rd:-
(a) On the front from the right to LA QUINQUE RUE by the 7th Divl. Artillery.
(b) On the remainder of the front by 46th Divl. Artillery.

Details of relief have been issued in separate instructions.

On relief the Divl. Artillery will march to the new area under Brigade arrangements.

G.O.C., R.A. 19th Divn. will hand over command of Artillery Groups at 10 a.m. on 22nd to G.Os.C. 7th and 46th Divl. Artillery.

TRENCH MORTAR BATTERIES.
4. No.11 Trench Mortar Battery will come out of the trenches with the 57th Brigade, and will be billeted in LOCON.

No.4 Trench Mortar Battery will remain in LOCON.

5.

NO.13 M.M.G. BATTERY	5.	No.13 M.M.G.Battery will come out of the line by sections, as the fronts which the sections cover are taken over by 7th and 46th Divns., and will proceed to the new area independently.
R.E. DETAILS.	6.	145th Coy.R.E. (Corps Troops) returns to XIth Corps H.Q. on 20th November; 187th Coy.R.E. is transferred to Ist Corps on 25th November.
MOVES.	7.	Necessary moves are shown in the accompanying March Table.
MEDICAL.	8.	Medical arrangements will be notified later.
COMMAND.	9.	G.O.C. 19th Division hands over command of the Divisional front as far as BOMB LANE to G.O.C. 7th Divn. on completion of the relief on night of 23rd/24th November. On night of 24th/25th November G.O.C. 19th Division hands over command of the remainder of the front to G.Os.C. 7th and 46th Divns., on completion of the relief.
REPORTS.	10.	Divl.H.Q. will remain at LOCON for the present.

[signature]

Lieutenant-Colonel,
General Staff.

Issued at 11-30 p.m.

Copies to:-
File.
War Diary.
G.O.C.
G.S.
A.A.&.Q.M.G.
G.O.C.,R.A.
C.R.E.
56th Infantry Brigade.
57th   ,,   ,,
58th   ,,   ,,
Divl.Cyclists.
187th Company R.E.

O.C.5th S.Wales Borderers.
Divisional Train.
M.M.G.Battery.
A.D.M.S.
XIth Corps.
Guards Division.
46th   ,,
7th   ,,
Divl.Signal Coy.
Divl.Squadron.

****

MARCH TABLE --- 19th DIVISION.

DATE.	UNIT.	FROM.	TO.	TIME OF MARCH.	ROUTE.	REMARKS.
Nov.22nd.	Reserve Bns. 56th Bde.	Present billets.	Between MERVILLE & FORET DE NIEPPE.	BRIGADE Arrangements.	LOCON -- PARADIS -- MERVILLE.	On relief by troops of 20th & 21st Bdes, which come under orders of 56th Bde.
" 23rd.	1 Bn.58th Bde. 2 Bns.58th "	LES LOBES. S.of LOCON.	Between MERVILLE and HAVERSKERQUE.	4-0 p.m. 4-0 p.m.	PARADIS -- MERVILLE AVELETTE -- S.bank of AIRE -- LA BASSEE Canal -- ROBECQ -- ST VENANT.	On arrival in Divisional Area of reserve troops 20th and 21st Bdes.
	H.Q.58th Bde. 1 bn.57th Bde.	W 6 d 3.6. RUE DE L'EPINETTE.	LE SART. LES LOBES.	4-0 p.m. --	RUE DU BOIS -- LES FACONS -- LE CASAN.	On relief by battalion of 20th Bde, which comes under orders of 57th Bde.
	5/S.W.B.	Present billets.	CORNET MALO.	9-0 a.m.	LE HAMEL -- LES CHOQUAL -- AVELETTE -- S.bank of CANAL -- PONT L'HINGES -- BOHEME -- QUENTIN -- CALONNE.	
	Divnl.Cavalry. " Cyclists.	-do- -do-	LA HAYE. ST FLORIS.	9-0 a.m. 9-0 a.m.	S.bank of CANAL -- ROBECQ. LES LOBES -- Q 30 b 5.9.-- PACAUT -- CALONNE.	
Night of 23/24th.	H.Q.56th Bde.	LOISNE.	W 6 d 5.6.	Brigade Arrangements.	-do-	On completion of relief of 56th Bde.by 20th & 21st Bdes. Troops in Reserve Bde. Area come under orders of 56th Bde.
	2 Bns.56th Bde.	Trenches.	S.of LOCON.	-do-	-do-	On completion of relief.

DATE.	UNIT.	FROM.	TO.	TIME OF MARCH.	ROUTE.	REMARKS.
Nov.24th.	Mobile Vet. Section.	LOCON.	P 11 a 6.6.	10-0 a.m.	AVELETTE -- S.bank of Canal -- ROBECQ.	
	Field Coys R.E.	Present billets.	RUE DES VACHES.	2-0 p.m.	LES LOBES -- Q 30 b 5.9. LE CORNET MALO.	
	2 Bns.56th Bde.	S. of LOCON.	Between MERVILLE and FORET DE NIEPPE.	11-0 a.m.	LOCON -- PARADIS -- MERVILLE.	
	H.Q.56th Bde.	W 6 d 3.6.	LES LAURIERS.	Brigade arrangements.		
	1 Bn.58th Bde.	LA TOMBE WILLOT.	Between MERVILLE & HAVERSKERQUE.	2-0 p.m.	PARADIS -- MERVILLE.	
	1 Bn.57th Bde.	LE TOURET.	LES CHOQUAUX.	--	RUE DU BOIS -- LES GLATIGNIES.	On arrival of Reserve Bn.20th Bde.
	2 Bns.57th Bde.	Trenches.	LA TOMBE WILLOT & S. of LOCON.	Brigade arrangements.		On relief by troops of 46th & 20th Bdes.
	H.Q.57th Bde.	CSE.DU RAUX.	W 6 d 3.6.	--do--	--do--	On completion of relief.
Nov.25th.	57th Bde.	LOCON Area.	ROBECQ.	10-0 a.m.	AVELETTE -- S.bank of Canal.	

APPENDIX I.

	To 7th Division.	To 46th Division.
FRONT SYSTEM.	LEES, GOLDNEY, KINKROO, LE PLANTIN E, FESTUBERT E.	ROPE, MARSDON, TUBE STA. LITCH.
CROIX BARBEE SYSTEM.	LE PLANTIN N and S, FESTUBERT, CAILLOUX (2), RUE DE L'EPINETTE W, TUNING FORK E and W, ROUTE A, LE TOURET E and CENTRAL, GORRE WOOD, LOISNE E and N.	CHAVATTES, LE TOURET N.E. RUE LE L'EPINETTE N.
ESSARS — BOUT DEVILLE SYSTEM.	LE HAMEL, LE HAMEL N.W., LAWE, LES CHOQUAUX	MESPLAUX N & W & E, LA TOMBE WILLOT.

19th Division No. 4/574/11

COPY.

1st Army No. 4/168/ AMS. 20/10/15.

  Cases have recently occurred of Officers Commanding units forwarding <u>recommendations for promotion in triplicate and duplicate</u>.

  This is quite unnecessary and undesired.

  It is hoped, therefore, that unit Commanders will be informed accordingly that they may be relieved of correspondence which is superfluous.

Headquarters   (Sd) S.C. Holland.
1st Army.   Captain.
                 A. M. S.

2.

O. Commanding 19th Divl Cyclists Coy.

For information and guidance.

H.Q. 19th Division.   Captain.
18th November 1915.   for D.A.A. & Q.M.G. 19th Division.

I. **Alterations in MARCH TABLE attached to 19th Division Operation Order No. 18 of 19th instant.**

November 23rd. Add:-

(1) 1 Battalion 58th Bde. from LA TOMBE WILLOT to between MERVILLE and HAVERSKERQUE; starting at 4.0 p.m. and marching via PARADIS and MERVILLE. Remarks -- " on arrival in Divisional Area of 138th Bde. of 46th Divn.".

(2) 1 Battalion 57th Bde. from LE TOURET to LA TOMBE WILLOT; marching via RUE DU BOIS -- LES FACONS -- LE CASAN. Remarks -- "on arrival of battalion of 138th Bde., which comes under orders of 57th Bde."

November 24th. Delete:-

(1) Move of 1 Bn. 58th Bde. from LA TOMBE WILLOT.

(2) Move of 1 Bn. 57th Bde. from LE TOURET.

(3) "LA TOMBE WILLOT &", in destination of 2 Bns. 57th Bde. moving out of trenches.

II. **Alteration in Appendix I of same Order.**

In accordance with XIth Corps No. R.H.B./392 of to-day, add MESPLAUX W. to list of works in ESSARS -- TOUT DEVILLE System to be handed over to 7th Division, and delete it from those to be handed over to 46th Division.

H.Q.19th Division,
20th November 1915.

Lieutenant-Colonel, G.S.,
19th Division.

Copies to:-

File.	O.C.5th S.W.Borderers
War Diary.	Divisional Train.
G.O.C.	M.M.G.Battery.
G.S.	A.D.M.S.
A.A.& Q.M.G.	XIth Corps.
G.O.C.,R.A.	Guards Division.
C.R.E.	7th Division.
56th Infantry Brigade.	46th Division.
57th ,, ,,	Divnl. Signal Company.
58th ,, ,,	Divnl. Squadron.
Divisional Cyclists.	

19ᵗʰ Bial: Gelebts
fol: 5

121/7884

Dec 1915

Army Form C. 2118

WAR DIARY
INTELLIGENCE SUMMARY
(Erase heading not required.)

Confidential

War Diary

of

the 19th Divisional Cyclist Company.

From 1st December To 31st December 1915.

VOLUME V.

WAR DIARY or INTELLIGENCE SUMMARY

Sheet 19

Place	Date	Hour	Summary of Events and Information	Remarks and references to Appendices
ST OMER	1.12.15		Drill marches etc. Coy & major drill. Coy Major Football v. 86th Bgde RFA and won. G.D. Night — no — takes out in direction of GARDEQUE and BOESNE. To diary.	
	2.12.15		Showery with high H.Q. guard the recruits arrived in the morning has as the "Onion Belens" arrived time hospital ship "Anglia" mined in the Channel. Coy M.H. bright & warm — paymaster to the field. Loren detach 7554 A.H. reported at E draw'g. ChFloor AQUETOIRE stuff — depôts adjutant. 3527 Pte Harris T. prompted	
	3.12.15		Foggy rain "Stand by" just of emergency detach. 48 hrs. Stores 4, 118 s.	Gen
	4.12.15		Very hot Cpl Smith Mf Harris get 20 cwt & x range rifles. Clothes washed. 4756 Pte Pinger to the research R.H.s lup. Pte Oley & two no reinforcement draft.	Hone
LOCON	5.12.15		Coy moved to LOCON. Gen billet in the town - cycles started in tobacco factory yard. Servicemen had been put back for leaving billets earlier so didn't into detach are ready for forest control officers. Drum & Fife out from for control too.	
	6.12.15		Very wet & stormy. The bomb returned from ROUSTON. CSM M. Hollis & seavadt. Hot. Coy sect of work on details in Rue Oubert. Lt. Bow Hobson + It Gabby Murphy.	
	7.12.15		Posted to CRE 9th div trainings officers. Right & Left brigade draw reflections. (attached 92nd 91st & 2nd Cav RE).	
	8.12.15		Coy out at FACTORY CORNER from 4pm to 10:30pm — working party to much safer at Rouge point night too foggy.	
	9.12.15		Not continuing to refuse - but much interrupted by shell fire. Left A + 2 off platz - the ditch filled the Canal out of thought. 6:30 Lyddite recruit from	

WAR DIARY or INTELLIGENCE SUMMARY

Army Form C. 2118

Sheet 20

Place	Date	Hour	Summary of Events and Information	Remarks and references to Appendices
LOOS	16/9/15		Coy holdes began burn of D. Batty. S.F.H. & R.F.A. Pireh at X9o45. West 36J working party from 9h 3.30 pm.	
	17/9/15		Continuous snow & a little rain. Coy moved 1 platoon continues on Inspection. 1 platoon to make a ditch in RUE DUBOIS. Rain & snow all pm.	
	18/9/15		Fine cold. Coy called out for urgent work on PRINCESS Road. Ditch moved from 4.30 am to 10.30 am. Rest of day in rest. 3858 F/f Platoon ordered as reinforcements for continuation on same work moving in 2 shifts. All day working at 4.30 am & 8.30 am. Het & fine. Stables on Thursday 50 yds & tells to incidents.	
	19/9/15		Sharp frost. Work continued in two shifts. Platoon to new full ditch with shafts 1 mar. & water pump in. R notice a shells falling on this ditch - some others being thrown & bridges. 3858 Lopt Centre encampts.	
	19/9/15		Sine men coys continued on ditch work & came on shift. Caroclogne number corps was heavily shelled today with 4.5 shrapnel shells went about 50 yds in this neighbourhood from 1 am to 4 pm.	
	20/9/15 21/9/15		Dull weather. Work continued as yesterday. Very little shelling. Only two platoons out today then from 9h 330. This rain poured heavily owing to the increased number of men going sick with chills. The doctor put it down to working too long in cold water. He also sees Hago got thoroughly chilled when working [Speaks?] to the platoon.	

WAR DIARY
INTELLIGENCE SUMMARY
(Erase heading not required.)

Army Form C. 2118

Sheet No 21

Place	Date	Hour	Summary of Events and Information	Remarks and references to Appendices
LOCON	16.12.15		Warm + wet slightly foggy. Only two platoons out today. Practically no artillery fire.	Fair
	17.12.15		Foggy all day. A.M.R. Posts relieved also Coy't Sons Grenad. Cold cloudy fine. Inspection of Smoke helmets, rifles etc. Coy paid out. Pte West in 13919 attached to Sanitary Coy hrs. Shot thro' the brain by a stray bullet whilst asleep in his billet at RICHEBOURG ST VAAST last night and reported to have 3no A.P. Butts. 41 and 13919 Pt melody (evacuated from M.A.C.	fair
	20.12.15 21.12.15		Warm + dull. Small working party out. Lull - hostile continued as previously. The CRE has decided that the Coy. Engs. will do work between the RUE DU BOIS and the firing line, and that attacks to Right Platoon's left Brigade front of Divisional area.	fair fair
	22.12.15		Continued "wet". Patrols out at night now, starting 8:30pm + getting back about 11pm. Right Platoon to Left Brigade front. Right working in the RUE DU BOIS, ALBERT FACTORY CORNER and Left N.9 LA BASSEE ROAD, on OXFORD ROAD (NEUVE CHAPELLE). The Right party were "W43" to go "over"; the Left Cam'n buries an old sap "nothing for fear of some trouble.	fair
	23.12.15		Dull cloudy - hard frost & Sleet. Posts out as before. Instructions drawn up for miller Secret instructions from OC Post Field Coy R.E.	fair
	24.12.15		Met Capt Paddy just as same from midnight - very unpleasant conditions. Col Edmonds Capt St. evacuated by MOTOR AMB. Pte Heaton & Coss join reinforcement.	See Appendix I
	25.12.15		Continued rain - wind but quite warm. Men had a Xmas Dinner at 12:30pm	Special Orders
	26.12.15		Change. Later Bailiffs apprise for Left cooks & orderly. Coy to Church Parade 9am Holiday	

WAR DIARY or INTELLIGENCE SUMMARY

Army Form C. 2118

Sheet 22.

Place	Date	Hour	Summary of Events and Information	Remarks and references to Appendices
LOCON	27.12.15		Heavy S. wind. Night parties out as usual time. 4156 Pte Perra J.P. joins as reinforcement.	Loan
	28 "		Brigadry Inspection by Major Genl Briggs CB, ASO Commanding 19 Division at noon. Passed in orders by CO. The CO would like to record in orders the result of the Inspection of the Bn. the Division today was by far much he appreciated the observation made by the General on the fine turn out of the Coy. He considers the reflects the highest "credit individually on all Officers, Warrant Officers, NCOs & men of the Coy". Both night parties out as usual. [Right] in NEUVE CHAPELLE near trenches ? — Left in RUE DU BOIS near FACTORY.	
	29 "		Continued Rainy S. wind. Nil occurred of any. Right Sector party out at 7pm — Left at 3.30pm — returned early on account of being badly shelled. 6.30pm Patrol from Left as reinforcement.	
	30 "		Quiet + warm, no wind. Bog. parties out in daytime — service at 10.30am. Strong close 4th[?] Left party worked on CHATEAU stick in NEUVE CHAPELLE. The Germans shelled the village very heavily. Patrol party driven away at 12.30am — did not return till 4.10am. — most of the time were spent in Court of Chateau in the village.	
	31 "		Still — Heavy S. wind. Working parties out at 1830 on Right party did not get to work till 11.35am. — Left to take orders from Kearny Felting (sumps) in EDGWARE ROAD, NEUVE CHAPELLE.	

Appendices III + I attached. M.D. 31/12/15

WAR DIARY
or
INTELLIGENCE SUMMARY

Army Form C. 2118

Appendix III

— Transport —

Information, Orders and Messages re Transport
of this Unit, 19 Bn. Ychief Company Summarized
by Lieut. J.C.S. WHITTUCK, 19 Divisn Ω Coy O.C.

Messages Sent & Rec'd

A.S. dated 30/7/15 from OC DCC to DHQ. "from average no. Could you arrange
"Supply wagon proceed here after (Lillers) refilling? Forward and wagons are not with A.S.C.
"train are wagons do not leave here till 2.30 p.m. forward afternoon and
"after refilling can proceed here to be loaded and march with our baggage
"wagon to LE SART" (MERVILLE. Ref. 36.a.)

Q. 141 dated 30/7/15 from DHQ. to OC DCC. "Reference from A S Coy re SC.
Q. 147 dated 1/8/15 from DHQ. to OC DCC. "The baggage wagon of the train total
"wagon Headquarters 1 Company today at NEUVILLEN for noload and recharge
"horses."

Letter dated 7/8/15 from DHQ to OC DCC. The Lt. M. Divisional Train has drawn
"attention to the very unsatisfactory way the horses of your baggage and supply
"wagons are looked after whilst they were with your unit. no less than three and
"The horses have had the places on the neck & back lost and recharged.
"This reveals a lamentable lack of horsemastership on the part of those responsible
"for your unit. In the care of the horses and to want of proper supervision on
"the part of being that the
"horses when with the unit are well cared for and that the wagons and accoutrements
"In reply to this letter it was pointed out that I have went neck there times
"and not three and of E three horses as stated. The Establishment of Transport for the
"Unit two inadequate for the necessary adjustments which it has proved.

Bn. 7/9/15 & copy D.A.F.G.1098-122. Instituting the Table field Repairs received of this Unit and
accessory to this Bn. Establishment was increased by 1 Cook's cart, 1 Draught horse and 1
horse. Q.237a. dated 14/9/15 from DHQ OH DCC. "Draw one L.P. horse from 19 Div. Am. Col.
"Q.30.6.5.9."

J.C.S.W

Appendix III, Sheet 2.

WAR DIARY
or
INTELLIGENCE SUMMARY
(Erase heading not required.)

Army Form C. 2118

A.47 dated 17/8/15 from O.C. D.C.C. to O.C. 154. Co. A.S.C. 19 D. Train. "This Company has once again tomorrow morning and kindly return the baggage wagon by 9 am."

A.73, dated 27/8/15 from O.C. D.C.C. to O.C. 154. Co. A.S.C. 19 D. Train. "As we are moving Sunday morning can you arrange for supply wagon to remain with us after delivering rations on Sunday."

A.151 dated 17/9/15 from O.C. D.C.C. to M.O. i/c 10 Lncs. Regt. "A number of my men are continually going sick into Ambulance undoubtedly due I thinking the water in natural state can could from report here are. I have been with length of time for the water — but in this Company and this sickness is no doubt due to the lack of this necessary article of Establishment" Copy to M.O. i/c 7 Eastern Bn.

Transport

Additional Summary by / Lieut G.H.M. MORRIS. 19th Div. Cyc. Coy 31/12/15.

D.R.O.g. H. Div. 28.12.15 No 582. "Transport". "While divisions are stationary, baggage, officers mess be concentrated with the O.C. Companies of the Train in accordance with L.11878, Statro. No 00041/1. all units will return their baggage wagons hence to the base. Copy of the Train on the 1st inst. Units requiring transport for any purpose will apply for same to O.C. Ant. Trans, LESTREM. N.R.O. notice should be given however possible.

From O.C. Div Train — M/226 – 22.12.15. "With reference to our conversation of this morning. I suggest that your Supply wagon cannot in future remain with your Coy. I would be glad if you will return it to the H.Q. Coy. of the Train tomorrow 23rd inst.

WAR DIARY
or
INTELLIGENCE SUMMARY

(Erase heading not required.)

Army Form C. 2118

Appendix V

Remarks and references to Appendices

Special Order of the Day. 25:12:15.
10th Division Cyclist Co.

The Commanding Officer would like to take the opportunity of this day being Christmas day to publish the few following remarks to the Officers, NCOs & men of the Coy. It is now just eight months since I had the privilege to command this Coy. During that long time I have had the opportunity to accompany the Coy. through many vicissitudes and to see them at almost every conceivable class of work rated to their legitimate work as Divisional Cyclists.

No Commanding Officer could possibly wish to command a finer, steadier or more straightforward body of men.

I wish to thank the Officers, NCOs & men generally for the excellent discipline which exists in the Coy. The general behaviour & deportment of all. When I was given the command of the Coy. it was impressed upon me by the GOC commanding the Division that the Divisional Cyclists should be a "corps d'elite" of the Division. I feel that without a doubt this has been easily accomplished and that there is not a finer body of men in the Division at the moment.

So nearly I wish the Coy. so long as we remain a Coy. the best of luck & every success. To Officers & men of Officers, NCOs & men. A merry Xmas & happy New Year & many happy returns. A merry Xmas & happy New Year & Victory & Peace

John J Hears
Capt

19th Division Order No. 19.

ORDERLY ROOM 3 DEC 1915 19TH DIV. CYCLIST Co.

R   Copy No.

3rd December 1915.

References to 1/40,000 Maps 36 A and BETHUNE Combined Sheet, and Trench Map.

Information	1.	The 46th Division is being withdrawn from the XIth Corps, and will be relieved in its portion of the line by 19th Division. Relief to be completed on the night of 4th/5th December.
Infantry 58th Brigade.	2.	(a) The 58th Brigade will relieve the 138th Brigade and the right battalion of the 139th Bde., on the front from QUINQUE RUE to COPSE STREET, both exclusive, on the night 3rd/4th December. The working party of 6th Wilts Regt. will move direct to the new Area.
56th Brigade.		(b) The 56th Bde will relieve the remaining Battalion of 139th Bde. and the 137th Bde., on the front from COPSE STREET (inclusive) to SIGN POST LANE (exclusive), on the night of 4th/5th December.
57th Brigade.		(c) The 57th Brigade will be in Divisional Reserve. Movements will be in accordance with the attached March Table. Details will be arranged direct between brigadiers concerned. Posts will be relieved by daylight; movements east of CROIX BARBEE --- LA COUTURE --- LE TOURET in small parties only, by day.
Artillery	3.	The 19th Divl. Artillery will relieve the Artillery of 46th Division on the nights of 3rd/4th and 4th/5th, under arrangements to be made direct between Divl. Artillery Commanders.
Other Reliefs.	4.	Other reliefs will be notified later.
Command.	5.	G.Os.C. 58th and 56th Brigades will take over command of their new Sections on completion of reliefs. The battalions of 138th and 139th Bde relieved by 58th Bde. in the trenches, and moving back for the night of 3rd/4th December to Brigade Reserve Billets, will come for that night under command of G.O.C. 58th Bde.; and similarly the battalions relieved in the trenches on night of 4th/5th December by 56th Bde. will come temporarily under the command of G.O.C. 56th Bde. The time and date when G.O.C. 19th Division assumes command of the new Divisional front will be notified later. Until then the 58th and 56th Bdes will be under the command of G.O.C. 46th Division.
Reports.	6.	H.Q. 19th Division remain at LOCON for the present.

A. Buckle
Lieutenant-Colonel,
General Staff.

Issued at 2-0 a.m.

Copies to :-
File.	56th Inf.Bde.	Guards Division.
War Diary.	57th " "	46th "
G.O.C.	58th " "	33rd "
G.S.	5/S.W.Borderers.	Div.Signal Coy.
A.A.& Q.M.G.	Divl.Train.	Divl.Squadron.
G.O.C.,R.A.	M.M.G.Battery.	Divl.Cyclists.
C.R.E.	A.D.M.S.	187th Coy R.E.
XIth Corps.		

MARCH TABLE -- 19TH DIVISION.
****

Date	Unit	From	To	Time of March.	Route.	Remarks.
3rd Decr.	1 Bn.58th Bde.	Billets	RUE DES CHAVATTES	9 a.m.	MERVILLE -- PARADIS -- VIEILLE CHAPELLE.	To rest in billets vacated by troops of 46th Division.
	1 " " "	"	RICHEBOURG ST.VAAST.	"	-do-	
	1 " " "	"	LACOUTURE and posts.	"	-do-	
	1 " " "	"	VIEILLE CHAPELLE.	"	-do-	
	56th Brigade.		Area LESTREM (exclusive) -- LES LOBES -- QUENTIN -- LE BOUZATEUX FME	11-0 a.m.	Brigade arrangements.	
Night 3rd/4th.	2 Bns.58th Bde.	RUE DES CHAVATTES and RICHEBOURG ST. VAAST.	Trenches.			In billets not occupied by troops of 46th Divn.

A March Table for the remainder of the reliefs will be issued later.

Copy No.

Addendum to 19th Division Order No.19.

3rd December 1915.

1. Further movements in relief of 46th Divn. are shown in the attached March Table.

2. The following movements are not shown therein :-

    (a) The 19th Divl. Train will exchange billets with 46th Divl. Train under arrangements to be made by Os.C. Trains.
    (b) Field Ambulances will exchange billets under arrangements to be made between the A.D.M.S. of Divisions.

    The above movements are to be arranged in such a way as to interfere as little as possible with the movements of other troops.

3. The 4th Bn. King's Liverpool Regt., from 46th Divn., is attached to 19th Divn. on relief of 46th Divn., and comes under G.O.C. Left Section for the present. The posts in this area (i.e., north or east of the following posts; HENS, BONES, GROTTO, ANGLE (all exclusive), VIEILLE CHAPELLE cross roads (inclusive) will be taken over from their present garrisons by ½ this battalion, now in Bde. Reserve, on 4th December; the remaining ½ battalion on relief in the trenches will go into Bde. Reserve.

4. Lists of trench stores handed over will be forwarded to Divl. H.Q.

5. G.O.C. 19th Division will assume command of the Divisional front at 11-0 a.m. on 5th December.

6. On completion of relief
    H.Q. Right Brigade will be at CSE. DU RAUX.
    "   Left   "   "   " " R 30 c 6.9.
    "   Reserve "   "   " " White House, VIEILLE CHAPELLE.

H.Q. 19th Divn. closes at LOCON at 11-0 a.m. 5th December and opens at LESTREM at the same hour.

Lieutenant-Colonel,
General Staff.

Copies to :-
  File.   5/S.W.Borderers.
  War Diary.   Divl. Train.
  G.O.C.   M.M.G. Battery.
  G.S.   A.D.M.S.
  A.A.&Q.M.G.   Guards Division.
  G.O.C., R.A.   46th   "
  C.R.E.   33rd   "
  XIth Corps.   Divl. Signal Coy.
  56th Infy. Brigade.   Divl. Cyclists.
  57th   "   "   Divl. Squadron.
  58th   "   "

MARCH TABLE -- 19TH DIVISION.

Date	Unit	From	To	Time of March	Route	Remarks.
4th Decr.	2 Bns.58th Bde.	Area LESTREM (exclusive) -- LES LOBES -- QUENTIN -- BOUZATEUX FME.	Area ST.VAAST -- CROIX BARBEE -- RUE DU PUITS.	9-30 a.m.	ZELOBES -- VIEILLE CHAPELLE -- road junction R 36 c 0.2.	Relieve reserve bns.137th Bde, and rest in their billets preparatory to moving into trenches.
	1 Bn.58th Bde.	VIEILLE CHAPELLE	RUE DES CHAVATTES.	9-0 a.m.	Bde. arrangements.	Relieving a Bn. of 138th Bde.
	1 " "	LACOUTURE and posts.	RICHEBOURG ST.VAAST and posts.	—	-do-	
	1 Bn.57th Bde.	Billets.	Between LACOUTURE and LE TOURET.	9-0 a.m.	PT.LEVIS, LOUCE CREME FME. -- S bank of Canal to AVELETTE -- LOCON -- MESPLAUX	
	1 " "	-do-	BOUT DEVILLE and LES 8 MAISONS.	"	road junction Q 9 a 0.1. -- QUENTIN -- PACAUT -- FOSSE.	Not to pass FOSSE before 11-30 a.m.
	1 " "	-do-	VIEILLE CHAPELLE.	"	Road junction Q 9 a 0.1. -- QUENTIN -- PACAUT -- ZELOBES.	
	1 " "	-do-	ZELOBES -- LA CIX. MARMUSE.	"	-do-	
	5/S.W.Borderers.	GORMET MALO.	LACOUTURE.	11-0 a.m.	CALONNE -- QUENTIN -- PACAUT -- ZELOBES -- VIEILLE CHAPELLE.	
	1 Fld.Coy.R.E.	RIEZ DU VINAGE.	X 5 c 9.6.	1-30 p.m.	Under orders of C.R.E.	Relieve Fld.Coys of 46th Divn.
	1 " "	-do-	X 5 b 5.4.			
	1 " "	-do-	R 36 a 7.7.			

Date	Unit	From	To	Time of March.	Route	Remarks.
Night 4th/5th Decr.	2 Bns. 56th Bde.	Area ST.VAAST -- CROIX BARBEE -- RUE DU PUITS.	trenches.	Brigade arrangements.		2½ Bns. 137th Bde. and 1 Bn. 139th Bde. replace these 2 Bns. in Bde.Reserve Area on relief in trenches and come under the orders of G.O.C.56th Bde. for the night
5th Decr.	2 Bns.56th Bde.	Area LESTREM (exclusive) -- LES LOBES --QUENTIN -- BOUZATEUX FRE.	Area ST.VAAST -- CROIX BARBEE -- RUE DU PUITS.	9-0 a.m.	ZELOBES -- VIEILLE CHAPELLE -- road junction R 36 c 0.2.	Relieving above Bns. 137th and 139th Bdes in Bde.Reserve.
	Divl.Cavalry.	LA HAYE	Q 18 c 8.3.	9-0 a.m.	CALONNE -- road junction Q 5 b.	
	Divl.Cyclists.	P 9 a 3.8.	LOCON.	"	--do--	
	No.13 M.G. Battery.	P 6 a 8.6.	New Area.	"		Position will be selected after reconnaissance.
	Divl.Ammn.Col.	J 21 a.	QUENTIN.	As convenient.	LE SART -- MERVILLE.	
	Bde.Ammn.Cols.			9-30 a.m.	ST.VENANT -- CALONNE.	

Copy No. 93

19th Division Order No. 20.

6th December 1915.

1. 56th Bde. will relieve 4th King's Liverpool Regt. in the posts in the Left Section on 7th December. On relief that battalion, less the detachment employed with 173rd Tunnelling Coy.R.E., will march at any convenient hour into billets about LOCON to be pointed out by A.A.&.Q.M.G., and will come under the orders of G.O.C. 57th Bde. in Divisional Reserve.

2. 2 Companies 5/S.Wales Borderers will move into the billets in RUE DU PUITS vacated by 4th King's Liverpool Regt.

3. No.4 Trench Mortar Battery is allotted for duty in trenches with 58th Bde., No.11 Trench Mortar Battery with 56th Bde.
No.66 Trench Mortar Battery remains in reserve at FOSSE.
No.67 Trench Mortar Battery, at present attached, in reserve, to 58th Bde., will move into reserve area under orders to be issued by A.A.&.Q.M.G.

Lieutenant-Colonel,
General Staff.

Issued at

Copies to:-
File
War Diary
G.O.C.
G.S.
A.A.&.Q.M.G.
G.O.O.R.A.
C.R.E.
56th Infantry Brigade.
57th ,, ,,
58th ,, ,,

5/S.Wales Borderers.
Divl.Train.
M.M.G.Battery.
A.D.M.S.
XIth Corps.
Divl.Signal Coy.
Divl.Cavalry.
Divl.Cyclists.

****

Copy No. 25

19th Division Order No.21.

9th December 1915.

1. 57th Brigade will relieve 58th Brigade in the Right Sector on the night of 11th/12th December. Details will be arranged between Brigadiers.

2. Garrisons of posts may be relieved during the day; no movement of formed bodies of troops East of the line CSE. DU RAUX --- COUR ST. VAAST before 4-15 p.m.

3. On relief of 58th Brigade, No.4 Trench Mortar Battery will be attached to 57th Brigade; and 4/King's Liverpool Regiment will come under orders of 58th Brigade, in Divisional Reserve.

4. G.O.C. 57th Brigade will take over command of Right Sector on completion of relief.

A.C. Buckle
Lieutenant-Colonel,
General Staff.

Issued at 10-15 p.m.

Copies to :-
File.	5/S.W.Borderers.
War Diary.	Divl. Train.
G.O.C.	M.M.G.Battery.
G.S.	A.D.M.S.
A.A.&.Q.M.G.	XIth Corps.
G.O.C., R.A.	Guards Division.
C.R.E.	33rd "
56th Infy.Brigade.	Divl. Signal Coy.
57th " "	Divl. Cavalry.
58th " "	Divl. Cyclist.

38th Division.

Secret.  Copy No. 25

19th Division Order No. 22.

17th December 1915.

1. 58th Brigade (including 4th King's Liverpool Regiment) will relieve 56th Brigade in the Left Sector on the night of 19th/20th December. Details will be arranged between Brigadiers.

2. Garrisons of posts may be relieved during the day; no movement of formed bodies of troops Southeast of the line ROUGE CROIX - LA COUTURE before 4.15 p.m.

3. On relief of 56th Brigade, No. 11 Trench Mortar Battery will be attached to 58th Brigade.

4. G.O.C. 58th Brigade will assume command of Left Sector on completion of relief.

Issued at 2-30 p.m.   Lieutenant-Colonel, G.S.,
                                 19th Division.

Copies to:-

File.	O.C.5th S.W.Borderers.
War Diary.	Divisional Train.
G.O.C.	M.M.G.Battery.
G.S.	A.D.M.S.
A.A.& Q.M.G.	XIth Corps.
G.O.C.,R.A.	Guards Division.
C.R.E.	12th Division.
56th Infantry Brigade.	Divisional Signal Company.
57th ,, ,,	Divisional Squadron.
58th ,, ,,	Divisional Cyclists.
38th Division.	

SECRET.   19th Division No. G.A.106/8.

O.C. Divisional Cavalry
 ,,   ,,   Cyclists.
H.Q. Divisional R.A.
 ,, 56th Infantry Brigade.
 ,, 57th   ,,   ,,
 ,, 58th   ,,   ,,
C.R.E.
O.C. 5th Bn. S.W. Borderers.

References to 1/40,000 Combined Sheet, BETHUNE.

The following is an extract from the Draft Defence Scheme for the Right Division of the XIth Corps, and is issued for information and guidance in the event of attack, pending the issue of the completed Defence Scheme.

ACTION IN CASE OF ATTACK.

*   *   *   *   *   *

ACTION BY TROOPS NOT IN TRENCHES.

(1) The Divisional Cavalry, if in billets, will move via L'EPINETTE to about LESTREM S (R 9 c 3.1.), clear of the main road; the O.C. reporting to Divisional Headquarters. The O.C. Divisional Cyclist Company will report to Divisional Headquarters by telephone from LOCON as soon as the Company has turned out.
If at work in the forward area, Divisional Mounted troops will form up and report to the nearest battalion H.Q. unless the tactical situation demands immediate action on their part.

(2) If at work in the forward area, the above instructions apply also to the ~~~~~~~~~~. If in billets they will form up at their alarm posts, the H.Q. and 2 Companies at LACOUTURE coming under the orders of the Right Brigade, and 2 Companies at BOUT DEVILLE under the orders of the Left Brigade, as Brigade Reserves.

(3) Working parties of Engineers, unless the tactical situation demands immediate action, will return to their billets, where units will remain in readiness to move as required.

(4) (a) The Garrisons of the works in the Front System in rear of the front line keeps will be reinforced from the battalions in Brigade Reserve up to the numbers considered necessary by Commanders of Brigades in front line.

   (b) The garrisons of the works in the CROIX BARBEE System -- except LE TOURET N.E., LE TOURET N., PENIN MARIAGE, CROIX BARBEE, and RUE DU PUITS -- will similarly be reinforced from the battalions in Brigade Reserve.

(5) After reinforcing garrisons of works as above, the remainder of the battalions in Brigade Reserves will be at the disposal of G.Os.C. Brigades in front line.

(6) The Brigade in Divisional Reserve (which must be held ready to move at 2 hours' notice) will move as follows:-

(a)

(a) If required to move into a position of readiness for action towards the right of the Divisional front (telegraphic order "concentrate right") it will assemble with two battalions on the continuous line of breastwork near the road X 17 central to X 5 d (KING'S ROAD), and two near the LE TOURET -- LACOUTURE road (EMPEROR'S ROAD).

Routes and positions.

(1) Battalion N of LE TOURET -- to southern end of KING'S ROAD via LE TOURET, its right on the RUE DU BOIS.
(2) Battalion at VIEILLE CHAPELLE -- via LACOUTURE, to north end of KING'S ROAD.
(3) Battalion at LES LOBES -- via road-junction X 1 d 7.8. -- bridge at X 8 central -- road junction X 8 b 8.3., to south end of EMPEROR'S ROAD.
(4) Battalion at LA CIX. MARMUSE -- via VIEILLE CHAPELLE -- X 4 central, to north end of EMPEROR'S ROAD.

(b) If required to move into a position of readiness for action towards the left of the Divisional front (telegraphic order "concentrate left") it will assemble near the continuous breastwork running from COUR ST. VAAST towards CROIX BARBEE, in the following order from the right--

(1) The battalion billeted at LES LOBES.
(2) ,, ,, ,, N of LE TOURET.
(3) ,, ,, ,, at VIEILLE CHAPELLE.
(4) ,, ,, ,, ,, LA CIX. MARMUSE.

Routes.

(1) From LES LOBES, via ZELOBES -- VIEILLE CHAPELLE -- LACOUTURE, to X 6 a. -- following (2).
(2) From N of LE TOURET, via LACOUTURE -- road junction R 36 c 0.2., to M 31 d.
(3) From VIEILLE CHAPELLE, via road junction R 30 c 1.8. -- military road from R 36 a 7.7. to R 31 a 4.4., to M 32 a.
(4) From LA CIX. MARMUSE, via FOSSE -- LES 8 MAISONS -- road junction M 20 c 2.2., to CROIX BARBEE.

(7) Each Brigade going into reserve will reconnoitre the above routes and forming-up places. Reconnaissance will also be made of the ground between the forming-up places and the front, with a view to advance across country for offensive action.

(8) The primary rôle of the Brigade in Divisional Reserve is counter-attack, to recover any part of the line that may have been lost. In the event, however, of a very heavy and successful hostile attack it may be necessary for the Brigade in Divisional Reserve to hold its ground in the CROIX BARBEE and VIEILLE CHAPELLE Systems pending the arrival of the Division in Corps Reserve. The G.O.C. the Brigade in Divisional Reserve will therefore be prepared, if necessary, to occupy the rearward works in the CROIX BARBEE System, named in para. 4(b) above, and the works in the VIEILLE CHAPELLE System. These will therefore be reconnoitred and preparations made for their speedy occupation if required.

H.Q. 19th Division,
16th December 1915.

A.B.Buckle
Lieutenant-Colonel, G.S.,
19th Division.

Copy No...25....

19th Division Order No.23.

25th December 1915.

1. The 56th Brigade will relieve 57th Brigade in the Right Sector on the night of 27th/28th December, under the usual conditions for safety. Details will be arranged between Brigadiers.

2. On relief of 57th Brigade, No.4 Trench Mortar Battery and troops of 38th Division attached to 57th Brigade for instruction will be attached to 56th Brigade.

3. G.O.C. 56th Brigade will assume command of Right Sector on completion of relief.

Lieutenant-Colonel,
General Staff.

Issued at 11-15 a.m.

Copies to :-
- File.
- War Diary.
- G.O.C.
- G.S.
- A.A.&.Q.M.G.
- G.O.C., R.A.
- C.R.E.
- 56th Infantry Bde.
- 57th " "
- 58th " "
- O.C.5/S.W.Borderers.
- Divisional Train.
- M.M.G. Battery.
- A.D.M.S.
- XIth Corps.
- Guards Division.
- 12th Division.
- Divl. Signal Coy.
- Divl. Squadron.
- Divl. Cyclist.
- 38th Division.

CONFIDENTIAL.

19th Division No: A/145/Z.

To:-
    Headquarters, 19th Divisional Artillery.
          "   19th Div. Royal Engineers.
          "   56th Infantry Brigade.
          "   57th Infantry Brigade.
          "   58th Infantry Brigade.
    O.C., 19th Divisional Cavalry Squadron.
    O.C., 19th   "   Cyclist Company.
    O.C., 19th   "   Signal Coy., R.E..
    O.C., 19th Divisional Train, A.S.C..
    O.C., 5/S.Wales Borderers (Pioneers).
    O.C., No: 13 Btty. Motor M.G. Service.
    O.C., 57th Field Ambulance, R.A.M.C..
    O.C., 58th   "   "   "
    O.C., 59th   "   "   "
    O.C., No: 36 Sanitary Section.
    O.C., 31st Mobile Veterinary Section.

    The D.A.G., 3rd Echelon, Base, has brought to notice numerous instances of Units failing to send in their monthly War Diary or rendering it in a very careless manner.

    The attention of all Units concerned is directed to Field Service Regulations, Part ii, Para. 140.. The Major-General Commanding trusts that Commanding Officers will give this matter their personal attention in order to prevent any further complaints from the D.A.G., Base.

H.Q., 19th Division,
26/12/15.

                         J.M. Davies Lieutenant-Colonel,
                         A.A. & Q.M.G., 19th Division.

19de Arb. Lychow
rst: 6
Tau

Army Form C. 2118

WAR DIARY
INTELLIGENCE SUMMARY
(Erase heading not required.)

CONFIDENTIAL

WAR DIARY
OF
19TH DIVISION CYCLIST COY.

from

1st January to 31st January 1916

VOLUME VI

WAR DIARY / INTELLIGENCE SUMMARY

Army Form C. 2118

Ref 23

Place	Date 1916	Hour	Summary of Events and Information	Remarks and references to Appendices

LOCON — Jan. 1st — Very heavy S. wind. Going very difficult. Both working parties out as usual. A fitt [?] m. Raining.

" 2. — Calm – warm. Inspected practice bayard. Stables. Afternoon football match v. "C" Coy. Styborn in form by Sgt 2nd Arris. + los – 4.3.

" 3. — Fine very easy Coy work. Working parties out as usual. 15071 Pte Elli. 1st Arris a reinforcement 7640 & 2/6th Arris arrived.

" 4. — Very windy – turned wet. Parties as usual – very quiet in forward area. Pte [illegible] Thomas shot through the head on the night 16–19 Dec. last is reported dead. He was buried in MERVILLE cemetery.

" 5. — Fine and very Sh-rainy. Working parties as usual. Instructions from D.H.Q. that 5th Brigade Pone to be reinforced in lyk S. Division Down. Lt Chalmers Sgn Post LINE to NEB SALIENT and Giolet's line to report tomorrow to Colonel CHOISY. (6th WORCESTER REGT. H.Q. in NEUVE CHAPELLE).

" 6. — 4.30pm — Continued windy. Coy Inspire & more out of Wilts into trenches. Leather Jerkins issued to all men. Send party left in Camp – oudias afternoon – no servants Q'in Stove etc with cooker attached to R.E. Coys. Lt HOBSON — Lt TALBOT in charge. 4 pm. Coy more to LT Morris — Divisional Aramig Officers will by LACOUTURE – in charge of Coy artificers. Cycles to Destrow at Brigade H.Q.

TRENCHES (NEUVE CHAPELLE) " 7. — Heavy rain – turned clear. Quiet, quiet day. Intermittent shelling – Fourviere Chateau Carriers with new Loves. Parades 5 IN Bs.

Army Form C. 2118

WAR DIARY
or
INTELLIGENCE SUMMARY
(Erase heading not required.)

Sheet 24.

Place	Date	Hour	Summary of Events and Information	Remarks and references to Appendices
In the Trenches (NEUVE CHAPELLE)	1/16 8am		Cold. Mr. wind. Coy in front line with 15th Worcesters. Frontage: OXFORD ST. to BREWERY RD. — men including 3 officers. O.M.S. appx at LES HUIT MAISONS (S.23.d. Sheet 36 contoured map). Transport & orderly room still at LOCON. CHATEAU hired. (Filled) & retaliation on our front line for our Trench Mortar.	R
"	9 "		Raining – thro fire. slight Mr. wind. Very quiet only artillery exchg. Occasional machine gun fire. traversing our parapets at night.	
"	10 "		Fine – N. wind. Intermittent artillery fire. Coy. stretcher-bearer brought by stretchers. Relief taken place as before. 6pm. Pte Hard 6448 killed – shot whilst marching back from front line along LA BASSEE ROAD by machine gun fire. (Opp. move into Reserve billets at LES HUIT MAISONS	
LES 8 MAISONS	"	6.30pm	by VIEILLE CHAPELLE (R30.a – about 36 contoured). 4756 Pte Pierce & men into also 6503 Pte Ellis. gun. Rifle & kit inspection.	
"	11 "		Very cold & sunny. Heavy N. wind. Much rifle/artillery fire. Men came to notice that whistle while very clear, could not be turned dull – rain later.	
"	12 "		French. Pte Taylor 1. was struck on the helmet (steel – 10th trench one) – this deflected the bullet & only caused a slight concussion. The helmet undoubtedly saved his life.	
"	13 "		Clear, keen, cold Mr. wind. – three Mr. rain midday. Rifle & smoke helmet inspection. Coy to point trenches night instruct. Pte Price E.C. 6474 evacuated.	
"	14 "		Cold & Mr. wind. Feet inspection Parade & move into Trenches. Coy occupied front line trench	
In Trenches	15 " 6pm		THE NEB Sabbath (from 1st STREET to BREWERY RD.)	
"	16 "		Dull & rainy – River day. Artillery activity on Right – DUKES Bn. Fire – cold. No. wind. A lull in operations. Enemy very quiet.	

WAR DIARY or INTELLIGENCE SUMMARY

Army Form C. 2118

Sheet 25.

Place	Date	Hour	Summary of Events and Information	Remarks and references to Appendices
IN THE TRENCHES	17.1.16		Cold & clear all mvt. Fairly quiet. Enemy still our rear defence works behind NEUVE CHAPPELLE. The night patrol found wire strong and no sign of enemy. Quiet all night.	
"	18.1.16		Wet & Snow very dull. Our front trenches into NEB shelled. One direct hit on a dugout. Pte Runnell hit - badly bruised in the leg. His rifle was completely smashed up. Active artillery retaliation & enemy front line. The enemy seemed very annoyed. More mit. D. order N°27 [sketch] Secret. Div. Comm.'s Brigade reserve night of the division relieved by 38th Division between 2/nd & 22nd int. Air relieve relation to recon morning 23rd & move to NEUVE ST VAAST P9a 38 [sketch] (continued Sheet 26) morning 25th.	
"	19.1.16	6pm.	Drive rather - nil 20th. Great aeroplane activity. Otherwise very little operation. Afternoon trench artillery duels. Hot quiet at night. Left for machine gun fire but more of it minority defeated. Pte G. N° Pinnell 10 r 3521 Lewis T evacuated. esophag Ellis. Report to reinforcement from XI Corps Rest Stn. Coy go back to reserve in Billets as before.	
LES RUIT MAISONS	20.1.16		Fine hot then not - very heavy Sh. rain. Rifle inspection only.	
"	21.1.16	9am. Noon	Coy received instructions from 57 Bge to return to billets at LOOSN. Inc a anti. all coy retained former billets.	

Army Form C. 2118

WAR DIARY
or
INTELLIGENCE SUMMARY
(Erase heading not required.)

Sheet 26.

Place	Date	Hour	Summary of Events and Information	Remarks and references to Appendices
LOCON	22.1.16		Fine, warm, little wind. Coy rano Baths at LOCON from 9am to 11am. O.C. 1 Lieut G.A. MORRIS got STEWART to arrange WRE's Rifle inspection. "Stand" at 2pm. 2003 Pte SMITH T and 4455 Pte CLUE J. evacuated on 20th inst.	Sam
"	23.1.16		Warm & dull. Inspection of general "clean up" in preparation to move into trenches.	
STEWART	24.1.16 25.1.16		Dull, cold wind from W. moved off at 9am to new billets PQA 910 (Armatiere Sheet 36) BETHUNE kept field & farm barns + lofts - horses & wagons in one - all in billets by comfortable for men. The .40 over from 28 Division in every unit & etc. Sam	
"	26.1.16		Warm & dull morning. Billets cleared - turned over 367 Pte Hughes J + 3579 farm Pte Healy J. evacuated 357 coy from R.A.M.C. for contagion boots.	
"	27.1.16		Continued dull. Raining starts. Physical drill & musket? Arm drill 9 - Rifle inspection also rifles + musketry Period. Route march 6-7 miles at 2pm fa...	
"	28.1.16		And Early Parade altered 8.7.30 on account of light drill at 9.30. Bridge .... joint practice at 11.30. Musketry drill etc in afternoon.	
"	29.1.16		Still + quiet warm. Capt. CHERBERT SMITH, go on leave leave 4 days. Musketry in morning + drill. Route march afternoon. Cpl. Bond to details & letters for instruction at the Anti-Gas School at PIPE on 31st inst Lieut. FV MYATT and Cpl HARLEY + Cpl Mills, started for School of Instruction at STEENVOORDE from Feb 1st. Rd. of CTLY Feb 26th 15.20 100013 p.m. at - Dantor R Grant return to Coy today - had any French guide...	

Army Form C. 2118

WAR DIARY
INTELLIGENCE SUMMARY
(Erase heading not required.)

Sheet 27.

Place	Date	Hour	Summary of Events and Information	Remarks and references to Appendices
ST. VENANT.	20.1.16		Colm rolls. Billet inspection & of Coy. etc. Buffet by O.C. Divine Service by Major Hockley. Chaplain to British Troops at 2 p.m. "B" Playd Sports at [?] (Officers at 3 p.m. in STEENBECK. Lost 3-1. Handicraft as usual by tedious & men in odd job. Control posts of "A" "B" "C" & "D" Coys. all down in front in the evening - were given by Infantry from	
"	21.1.16		Col. A. McBush. M. Brig. Inspected (1) 26.1.16 with a General Absence. The whole Coy. was thoroughly and carefully inspected at 10 am. Brushing and of morning. Proved most of for 2 hours in afternoon. Some had a heavy contingent tournament Zone fair have been loaned for 3 days in succession.	

WAR DIARY
INTELLIGENCE SUMMARY

(Erase heading not required.)

Army Form C. 2118

CONFIDENTIAL

WAR DIARY
of
19TH Division Cyclist Coy.

From 1st to 29th February 1916

VOLUME VII

including Appendix VI

WAR DIARY / INTELLIGENCE SUMMARY

Army Form C. 2118

Sheet 28.

Place	Date 1916	Hour	Summary of Events and Information	Remarks and references to Appendices
SUZANNE	Feb 1		Coln. Fire. Coy. attached to from Kings at 7.25a. No one from the 8 Cos. lay down in K.25.c. only three from 5 min. at work. Application - average fire effect. Also fragments these but no Can't dy commence firing the force. 6504 Pte Barnes (C discarded 28.16 and 5037 Pte Davis Percents personals disorganised.	
"	"2		Very Cold + fine. 6035 Cpl Stephenson H. 3199 Pte Curby J. 3140 M. Parry J. Jn. as reinforcements from 1103 Infty Base Depôt. Posted to No.2 platoon. Orders to say lost 20 OR's March - recently few 1.16 3 Army Training Area - turn about COHEN and FLECHIN - Rte about 14 miles - Resting from 9.30am to 3.30pm. About 20 men fell out, not large.	
"	"3		14 Cases of which were cycle trouble. Cold + fine. Strong N. wind. Coy. (less overland) charging 5 cycles of appointment & faults. Platoon's yesterday + cycles put in order. Football match at 2pm Platoon v. Coy. NCO's on the Rifles 3&2 Pte Smith T. + L/Sgt Pte Connor Jn. as reinforcements from	
"	"4		Wet + cold. Field day afternoon Inspection of men turned out by Coy NCOs before taken to billet - Route March in afternoon	
"	"5		Wet turning fine. Parade inspection on the Platoon C. Also at. Coy. Practice use of helmet - Coy. drill. Recreation- football + afternoon.	
"	"6		Fine cold. Strong. Rifle inspection. Payment. Football C. Coy v. 8th Glosters - Coy. how Q-1. 4452 Pte Haleh. 11467 Pte Hollis On. 3317 Pte Cork J. L. 6035 Cpl Stephenson H. 4039 Pte Spencer A. 4453 Pte McGlone A. evacuated.	

WAR DIARY

INTELLIGENCE SUMMARY

Army Form C. 2118

Sheet 29.

Place	Date 1916	Hour	Summary of Events and Information	Remarks and references to Appendices
STEENWERCK	Jul. 7		Fine - turning train heavy S.H. and. Physical drill 930-735. Parade 930am. Monts march to RELY. Sol-FRE. Platoons then Sgt Mars by different routes as patrols french. STEENWERCK a roman hostile - as a hoplinendry & top exercise often.	
"	"8		hot-sunny. 730 Physical drill. 8.15 1115 Platoon have baths returns clothing rebills - these blankets were disinfected as they were found the lorry owing to a mixup in reissues of blankets. 930 Riot of Coy 90 in around Pointe Marcel State in afternoon. 4 pm Lecture by Bricks. Thursday today 2NCOs + 18 men Parade at BHQ - not as a "Stars" attack or trench against a bombing party. The party went (6 Tomorrow. All this week 2NCOs + 8 men of the Bats HEADS or ISBERGUES O.5c 5D (Sher36A) Road 5w6 from R.E. The O.C. has admitted to N°2 London Cavalry clearing hospital MERVILLE into an accident to this knee.	fine.
"	9		Fine + dull. Coy out for a funel Route March - ROBECQ - LINGHAS - GUARBECQUE - STEENANT. DES CARTS + Milner Rd, report for motor lorries from 58 FA. G) MAYO Boatrom Team of 8 Gustners shot Mun 4 - 1.	m.
"	10		Fine well long route march (Bat) ROBECQ - ANCHY - RELY - ESTREE BLANCHE - GUARBECQUE - St about 8am full out - back at 8pm	fair.
"	11		very strong N. mind + rain Instruction of min Rifle. Lecture K NCO on Guide 3nd Pte Larter of pecs in Lonbecker + from hospital.	fair.

WAR DIARY
INTELLIGENCE SUMMARY
(Erase heading not required.)

Army Form C. 2118.

Sheet 30

Place	Date 1916	Hour	Summary of Events and Information	Remarks and references to Appendices
STEENWERCK	12/12		Very wet & strong wind. Cycle cleaning. Nos 3 & 4 McDonald, Hodgkin Spencer & rejoin Coy as reinforcements from hospital.	fair
"	" 13		Wet & cold. Coy. rifle inspection 9 a.m. Church Parade in field 10.15 a.m. (CME) RC etc Church at ST. MAURICE. Coy the inoculation, but only temporarily sends for this purpose 6 men reporting the inoculation took place at 5 p.m. at 5 R Dgs R.O.B.G.C.Q. After employment were not taken. Instructors received from D.H.Q. the "Division & returning & take over line again". - Reft. Sector 58th Div. & right accept Guards Divn — W. Coy. la front. ... Détach Bn. platoon.	fair
"	" 14		One High wind. N to S.W. Coy. of Arty after inoculation. Div. School finish. & Lieut. Knott + 2 Corporals return to Coy. O.C. returns to Coy. from Hospital at MERVILLE. Lieut. HASKEW to LESTREM to arrange billets as Coy receive instrs to move (en 14 mls.). See FGP Contents N. rejoins Coy from 19 S Rfly Base Depot.	fair
"	" 15		Awl. High Sh. m. hind. Lieut. GIBB goes to 19 K Div. train for a few days re his transfer to M.T. a.s.c. Note mist kind. Lieut. MOLLUIST (Lt. DALHOUSIE?) arr. CRA ST Corps on the Transfer to RGA. Arrn taken rather badly over inoculation.	fair
"	" 16		Very heavy N. wind & rain. Pte HASSALL to hospital re inoculation. Lieut. HODGSON goes to take over billets from GUARDS Divn. Cyclists (LESTREM) with Advance Party to occupy & prepare billets.	fair

NOTE. The duplicate copy of this DIARY of Movements was sent to O. F. ACC records. HOUNSLOW — Origl per Lt. Capt. Infy to Xmonday 31.10.15(?)

WAR DIARY or INTELLIGENCE SUMMARY

Army Form C. 2118

Sheet 31.

Place	Date	Hour	Summary of Events and Information	Remarks and references to Appendices
S. VENANT. LESTREM	Sept. 17	9am	This ADMS moved off at 9 am. via usual track - MERVILLE - Fullet in forms over Canal N.S. village - took over from QUIRKE. DIV CYCLISTS. Capt. arrived in Ambulance.	Sam
		10am	Very wet muddy. Improvement of billets. We have to retain APMs post; scullery through the area. Slight purchases for mens toilet. Party of 20 men detailed daily for CRE including state from fly carts dump.	Sam
"	" 18			Sam
"	" 19		Quiet my cold. Inbounding Batty as before. Pont du HEM existing but restored daily. Billet rifle inspection. MOTOR PLOCE (G.S.O.2) Came here about trench guide from men he provides (2/M men to pts. Kerr, Alphonse, Smith S, Barker) handed to accom H. Inspected T.1102 London Cleaning	Sam
"	" 20		Bright - rime. Rifle & Helmet inspection. Pay out. Clothing issue. Reports the permission to CRE on condition of certain roads in ArtY area which needs repairs. The following men reported from hosp. duty. Base Depots. 868 Sgt. Burst, 1/1, 1213 Pte Butter 9, 937 Pte Doyerty J, 965 Pte Doherty J, 730 Pte Neville N, 9009 Pte hate R, 1090 Pte Hamm W, 459 Pte Taylor J were posted to sections. No.5 Hays Pleto at Gorthous - Show 31.	Sam
"	" 21		My cold. Left on Reason about 5 Apm. in whorry to S. Pol. movement of civilians critic. - Aircraft - LABOURSE - HINGETTE - PONT DU HEM - LESTREM - JULE CAMPBELLE - BEIY DIFFICILE which a search has ordained for Govt. property and carried by organs. Officer a D. NCO the details of this a school of instruction at DMO in set. notes	Sam

(J.T.14667 — Sch. Prot. — Col. D. service details)

1875 Wt. W593/825 1,000,000 4/15 J.B.C. & A. A.D.S.S./Forms/C. 2118.

WAR DIARY / INTELLIGENCE SUMMARY

Army Form C. 2118

Month: Feb 1916

Place	Date 1916	Hour	Summary of Events and Information	Remarks and references to Appendices
LESTREM	Feb 22		Cold, clear. Zeppelin 1000 men short A.P.M. — 30 men returned — others from Examining Post won't let 60 R.A.D.E. while it is in session. Unloading parties. Gain 2 pm. Zeppelin shows fall at 10.30 am — carried on all day. Coy N from H.Q. 9 hrs apart 4 Hrs + 25 men. Capt. Smith goes on leave. Following reports re reinforcements from H.Q. Rifle Bde Report 5740 Cpl. McGann E, 930 Pte Preston A, 3576 Pte Hucker J, 3820 Pte Payne I, Pte Barham L, Notes re absence. Pte to Stephens B, 8594 Pte Jennings B, Notes re absence. Hard frost pm.	
"	"23		Hard frost. Appn shown. School of Instruction Cancelled. Infantry Reports C.R.E. for road & Right Section (191st Leicester G. R.E.). Sects engaged in Entertainments at LAGORGUE Fty. GHQ Concert Troupe. (5 off. 100 men). 11 officers & 30 men to NEUVE CHAPPELLE for H.Qrs. "Search parties." Unloading parties as usual for C.R.E.	
"	"24		Very cold indeed. 14° of frost in the night. Low men for C.R.E. — dumps, determination tramway etc. 30 to A.P.M. and 30 to miscellaneous fatigue outside the Coy. Lieut. G.A. Morris with Nos 4 & 6 Platoons detailed for O.C. No 6 R.E. in Right Sectn drainage — but weather conditions make work impossible. Gun.	
"	"25		Continued hard frost. 15°–20° frost in the night. Tramway H.R.E. parties out. Heavy fall of snow from 4.30 pm. Owing to Unmarch for men beyond the strength of the Coy, a statement of Employment has gone to C.R.E. See Appx VI work well carried. Gun.	

Army Form C. 2118

WAR DIARY
INTELLIGENCE SUMMARY
(Erase heading not required.)

Sheet 33

Place	Date 1916	Hour	Summary of Events and Information	Remarks and references to Appendices
LESTREM	26.2		Continued very cold — hard frost — Heavy snowfall in night. Instructions issued to all officers & NCOs details for Div¹ School of Instruction to attend at MERVILLE on Monday 28th inst. Damage done in tornado. Int. Gum-Boots. Thigh Ft. drawn from 57th Bde. H.Q. Loading party to be to CRE for ration dumps. Spearmint. Tramway party. 20 men. Sandbag from CRE that remainder of men of Coy. not otherwise employed be placed at disposal of OC 9th Field Coy RE. This in reply to statement of strength sent yesterday.	
"	27.2		Dull & thaw set in very quickly. NCOs in charge of section of tramway area went out to inspect their section — hope should be possible tomorrow. Inspection of Coy by Lt Col. No 3867 Pte Hughes & rejoins coy as reinforcement. Additional men arrived this drawn from 57th Bde. H.Q.	
"	28.2		Warmer & duller — Lieut Armitage & 2 Rifle Scott (PLUM ST & SIGNPOST LANE) proceed in 6 section - arranged (summary?) reporting daily to OC Pk Bells Co. loading parties as usual. Officer & 2 NCOs detailed for Div¹ School of Instruction. 8524 Pte Austen C. 10480 Pte Proctor W. H.| Gillman C. 8705 Angel E. form as reinforcements.	
"	29.2		Heavy very bright. Tomorrow draw up. CREs instructions received for Report to ZIMENTIE tomorrow to OC B² 2nd Bedfs to RE for urgent work. In algo ordered for 20 men at 9:30 am + 30 men at 1:30 pm – loading parties.	

WAR DIARY
INTELLIGENCE SUMMARY   APPENDIX VI.
(Erase heading not required.)

Army Form C. 2118

Statement of Employment of men of 19th Div. Cyclist Coy.
Prepared for the information of the CRE 19th Div.
under date 25.2.16. by G. HAM MORRIS Lieut.

Permanently Employed

Details	Off.	men
with Coy.		27
" Salvage Coy.	1	5
" Corps French Tramways		2
" Forest Control Duties	1	2
Trench Guides D.H.Q.		7
Batmen not with Coy.		3
D.H.Q. Signal orderlies		6
" Guard		32
Details & O.C. 94 C.R.E. (Armentieres)	1	40
" Loading parties — C.R.E.		20
" Dump LAGORGUE "		10
	2	154

Temporarily Employed

Leave .... 1 ... 3
Experimental Trenches } 1 . 40
under R.E.
                          2 . 43

Effective Strength of Coy.
8 officers
198 men

Capt. J.S. 2.'16

19. Co

Formed 18.1.15
Stationed at Bulford
  Left Bulford 17-7-15
  Arrived Havre 18-7-15
   "   Hingette 31-8-15
Carried out Field Training etc.
     Furnished Guards & working parties
Same routine till 31-10-15

C 125

From, O.C.
    19th Division Cyclist Coy.
To   The Officer.
    I/c A.C.C Records
      Hounslow Barracks.

Reference your E/20139 dated 29.10.15.
Respecting your detailed headings for information required concerning this Company.

    Most of the information asked for is given in our War Diary, a copy of which will in due course reach you. The original is sent every month to the D.A.G. The Base and a duplicate is sent to you.

The following is a short precis.

(I) This Company was formed 18.1.15.

(II) It was composed of transfers from every line battalion in the Division with the exception of the Pioneer Battalion. Being an average of 23 N.C.O.s. men from each battalion.

(III) The Company was originally formed at Burnham, Somerset. in billets, and moved from there to Sling Plantation, Bulford 27.4.15. It left Bulford for service overseas on 17.7.15. It arrived at Serques near St. Omer France on 20.7.15. It left there on 23.7.15 arriving at Lillers on 24.7.15. It left Lillers on 31.7.15 arriving at Merville the same day. The Company remained at Merville one month. The Division having been attached to the Indian Corps. This Company left Merville 31.8.15 arriving at Hinge near Locon the same day. It has been at this place since, with the exception of 18 days

when the Division moved.
(IV) The Company have been engaged in working in the forward area since 2.9.15. It has been attached to the R.E. and is carrying out various works under the C.R.E.
(V) No officers have either been killed or wounded in this unit. Neither has any officer or soldier distinguished himself in action.
One officer has been transferred to the R.E. and one officer seconded to the R.E.
Two officers are attached to the R.E.
One officer is seconded to command the Divisional Salvage Company
(VI) No drafts have been received sufficiently strong enough to form an officer's party. One officer and several men have been received on drafts since our arrival abroad.
(VII) This Company has had 1 officer and 11 N.C.O's and men evacuated. It has received 1 officer and 6 N.C.O's & men as reinforcements. It has 35 N.C.O's & men permanently detached to form Divisional Headquarter Guard, and 9 N.C.O's and men to form part of Divisional Salvage Coy.
This Company has also undertaken traffic control duties under the A.P.M. of the 19th Division. These men are not permanently detached from the Company and are relieved at various intervals.

Herbert Smith
CAPT.,
O.C. 19th DIV. CYCLIST CO.

4.11.15.

Army Form C. 2118

WAR DIARY
or
INTELLIGENCE SUMMARY
(Erase heading not required.)

Confidential

War Diary
of
19th Division Cyclist Company.

from 1st to 31st March. 1916.

Volume VIII.

19 Div
Cyclists
Vol 8

WAR DIARY or INTELLIGENCE SUMMARY

Army Form C. 2118

Sheet 3A.

Place	Date 3/16	Hour	Summary of Events and Information	Remarks and references to Appendices
LESTREM	March 1st		Warm fine. Lieut G.A. MORRIS and 4 prom. Cpls & out. drainage right sector. Application for transfer to A.S.C./M.T.	
"	" 2.		Storey and 6 to party at LAVENTIE & tube are forward attached R.E. 2nd to R.E. for works in Left sector - drainage &c. Col. Peter tried by one General Court Martial for neglect while in charge of guard - found guilty - & reduced to Ranks. P. first Smoke helmet (with mica eye pieces) issued to Capten J. Watson. Of LESTREM. S&S Pte Lewis P. from asking removal on D.S. No. 3607 Pte Hughes J. from Siege F38 Div. A.G.	
"	" 3		Dull & rainy. Duties continue as previously. S&S Cpl Castells transferred to 33 Div. A.C.G. Captain Smith's leave extended 48 hrs.	
"	" 4		Snow, very cold. Party from 9th & 2nd R.E. Lieut.; RICHEBOURG - CASSOLUS to move by lorry to Siege to R.E. - carrying bombs for the Howitzers. The Cooks Cpl. Redman could not take wrongly out of use. Pass Pte Austin C. granted	
"	" 5		Changeable weather. Snow & Storms. Coy. Payout & Kit Insp. LAVENTIE party. A & S R.E. part had to come up for more to commence drainage of an area in the N.E.B. which appear likely to being reclaimed by 4th F.L. works. Adv. Pte Cox & Engineer as a munition worker to Gramophone 6.3.16	

Army Form C. 2118

WAR DIARY
or
INTELLIGENCE SUMMARY
(Erase heading not required.)

Sheet 35.

Place	Date 1916	Hour	Summary of Events and Information	Remarks and references to Appendices
LESTREM	March 6		Northerly front. L/Cpl Haynes A/Cpl to Commander R.H.D.S.S. 19 Div. No Parties made Like (unpaid) went to No 3 Platoon ment at LAVENTIE. No. Guard party on stake to the Cycle coster. Pte T. Leigh R/fd to Divisional Band - Lebourz... Lewis & Price Ec. brought in reinforcement from HQ 9/11 Bde Brae 11/6/15.	
"	" 7		Fine Cold. Drainage party out - Party at LAVENTIE on road by R.E. & any odd job. 9 men to sick - Cpl. Ho etc	
"	" 8		Very hard snow in the morning, but brilliant Sunshine - Quick thaw. The drainage pte went out at midday - Lieut. HOBSON sent a Pioneer Captain in 3rd A.W. with office & drainage in Area PLUM St - QUINQUE RUE S (5-21. Built 36 BETHUNE). Forge again at night ???...	
"	" 9		Frost - Thaw later. Tried in attach two to get camp for the men at night, but no on successful for but 3 days. Cpl. Gaan Constructed a good field oven for cooking, fine.	
"	" 10		Snowed & thawed. Work Continues on drains - great quantity of water flowing during the melting snows.	
"	" 12		Rain. Cold. Drainage parti have a day of rest for attending to netting of an Guard economy & Inspection of equipment, Rifles, knives to etc. Stable.	
"	" 11		Same milk. A/Lt. drowning in CHURCH ROAD - NEUVECHAPELLE today a couple found on Montyman drowned. He has been missing in the 1/7 the attack of the front Line. Artificial Respiration tried but of no avail.	

1875 Wt. W593/826 1,000,000 4/15 J.B.C. & A. A.D.S.S./Forms/C. 2118.

WAR DIARY or INTELLIGENCE SUMMARY

Army Form C. 2118

Sheet 36.

Place	Date	Hour	Summary of Events and Information	Remarks and references to Appendices
LESTREM	Mar. 13		Fine & warm. Enemy's work continued. Party at LAVENTIE shelled in forward area. 83rd Lift took H.E. evacuated to No. 107 Casualty Clearing, MERVILLE on 13th inst. The enemy sprung a mine at THE DUCK'S BILL from N.Q NEUVE CHAPELLE early in the morning and did much damage. During the morning the enemy shelled the sector very heavily & with gas shells (lacrymatory). The men working in trenches LIEUT KNOX and SJT. AYNESLEY in the area came under the gas & suffered much discomfort but only two went sick.	
"	14		Fine & warm. Afternoon 90° battle at LA GORGUE after work in trenches. Evening burn of drain in the NEUVE CHAPELLE sector about 11 a.m a warning was sent along to expect gas and at one time the filter had passed to put on helmets and all turn out. The wind was right but strong. All passed off.	
"	15		Some rain. E.winds. Clear & heavy (Riding in forward area. About Retaliation for the affair at the DUCK'S BILL (see 13th inst.) — heavy artillery. An alarm of a gas attack sounded by H.Q. at about 11.30pm all ranks were warned to be prepared & take necessary precautions. The civilian population (civilians) were also warned.) No gas reached No however. It is thought there has been trouble down around the line.	
"	16		Rain & cher. Shelling in both sectors. Much repairing of damage done & trench instructing Neuve Chapelle. Army yesterday 6 tonight through NEUVE CHAPELLE.	

WAR DIARY
INTELLIGENCE SUMMARY

Army Form C. 2118

Sheet 37.

Place	Date	Hour	Summary of Events and Information	Remarks and references to Appendices
LESTREM	May 17		Fine many clouds. Work as usual. Find all day ammr Pres E. Irtolight to gun. Strong for enemy gun.	
"	18		Dull morn, rain later. Huns still in E.S.E, moving South. We tried our gas alarm. Syds. at (Duidlam) in NEUVE CHAPELLE sector. The enemy took my little notice, but the section had to move out as it was shelled.	Puy.
"	19		Fine & warm. Inspection of clothing and pay out EH	
"	20		Brighter warm. Cpl Waterfall dipl little went on leave; Ptes Ball.) Corbin returned from Field Ambulance EH	
	21.		Dull & cold. Pte Blood attached Div. train. Lt Aynsley, Pte Leigh went on leave. Lt Knott killed by stray shell on RUE BACQUEROT. Sgt McManus, Ptes Barrett & Slany wounded, and Stuck ?/ EH except 1 NCO of Manus. Still rainy to withdraw detachment with 82 ?/c R.E. Lt Knott buried B.B. Arranged to withdraw detachment of Sgt McManus, Ball & Pte Blackburn	
	22.		PONT DU HEM cemetery. Gallant conduct of Sgt McManus reported to Division EH Pte T. Morris returned from leave.	
	23		Dull. Rain. Visited left B. LEFT SECTOR. Indented for timber for feeding totter. Saturday's and to be allotted to field training. Capt Smith struck off Strength 7 Coy from 13. 3. 16 EH Lt Talbot returned from School of Musketry.	

WAR DIARY or INTELLIGENCE SUMMARY

Army Form C. 2118
Sheet 38.

Place	Date	Hour	Summary of Events and Information	Remarks and references to Appendices
LESTREM	24.3.		Heavy snow. Lts Moilliet, Munro, Sgt Evans, Cpl Blackburn & L/Cpl Carter went on leave. L/ Talbot and 40 men required for coal fatigue Merville. Pte Barrett died on 23.3.16. Buried MERVILLE on 24.3.16. Visited drains 27-42. Very quiet. Went to see C.R.E. re rakes. B4	
	25.3.		Bright v fine. M. Sick 5 M & D. Left platoon failed to reach rendezvous on acct. of shelling. Much water from snow. Drew boots by Lt Talbot HINGES. 5 sheets BETHUNE COMBINED sent from HQ. Sgt Newton, Pte Jerry went on leave. Feeding tables completed. B4	
	26.3		Cold and wet. Inspection of arms in billets. Patrol went out on left. No 1. went baths. B4	
	27.3.		Fine occasional showers. W. wind. Visited 33-44. Some sniping. Took over recreation hut from 35th Div. Cpl Chester & L/Sgt Bowen 27.3. Sent cheque 65 frcs Lloyds (PRI) for cash duck magnet. B4	
	28.3.		Dull, cold. Drew 700 frcs HINGES. Sgt Bond granted special leave. Stocked recreation room from B.E.F. canteen MERVILLE by cheque on PRI. Work as usual. B4	
	29.3.		Bright v fine. High wind W. Sgt Bond, Sgt Randall, Pte R.F. Roberts went on leave. Cpl Petch replaces Sgt Randall in charge of detachment with 82nd R.E. Sent FOSSE for timber. Visited STILLELOYE.T. 2/Cpl Oxley evacuated. Cpl Karzyski's cycle lost. 8 men paraded D.H.Q. for inspection by G.S.O.2. Handed over recreation hut and stock (including sayer stove) b - 3 - 9 - 2 m Paid 32 Cpls. 10 Wks 5frcs each. Monthly bills approved. Inventories of kits taken by Lt Talbot of kits of Capt Smith & Lt Knott & Lt Knott & men left to finish some work between 44 42. B4	

Army Form C. 2118

WAR DIARY
or
INTELLIGENCE SUMMARY Sheet 39
(Erase heading not required.)

Instructions regarding War Diaries and Intelligence Summaries are contained in F. S. Regs., Part II. and the Staff Manual respectively. Title Pages will be prepared in manuscript.

Place	Date	Hour	Summary of Events and Information	Remarks and references to Appendices
LESTREM	30.3.		Fine & cold. Ptes Morgan, Taylor B.S. chosen as trench guides. Work as usual. BH	
	31.8.		Heavy mist early. Pte dt Talbot, Pte Midwinter went on leave. Lt Aproby returned from leave. Work as usual. BH	
	1.4.		Fine & warm. Field training. Outpost scheme. Sgt Evans, L/Cpl Carter returned from leave. L/Cpls Haynes & Pte Baker. BH	
	2.4.		V/fine & warm	

Army Form C. 2118

19 Div Cyclist
Vol 9

WAR DIARY
or
INTELLIGENCE SUMMARY
(Erase heading not required.)

CONFIDENTIAL

WAR DIARY
of
19TH DIVISIONAL CYCLIST COY.
from
1st ⊕ to 30TH APRIL 1916

VOLUME IX

WAR DIARY
INTELLIGENCE SUMMARY
(Erase heading not required.)

Army Form C. 2118

Sheet 40.

Place	Date	Hour	Summary of Events and Information	Remarks and references to Appendices
LESTREM	1916 1 Apr		Fine, warm. Field training; outpost scheme. Two applications for transfer to AOD - Lepl Haynes & Pte Baker.	
	2 "		Very fine, warm. Coy. field ont. Fatigue party from the EPINETTE dump returned. Capt C.A. Smithe + Lieut T.V. Knolls kits sent to MERVILLE.	
	3 "		Fine, warm. Parties as usual in forward area on drainage work in STILLE LOY CT. 65ft from LLOYDS bombing MG Gun.	
	4 "		Dull & chilly. O.C. Capt. HOBDEN out at Bishop & arranging work for softy party on MORTED GRANGE ST for night. Arrangements for recreation. Boxing. Clone for night. LIEUT. MORRIS did not return from leave - on between Divns. Promoted.	
	5 "		Fine cold. 102 Platoon on M.G. CT - Syft, working party cancelled as no reaping hooks available.	
	6 "		Fine, scott. 2 Platoons now on M.G.CT. but still no Rosko Rle & stand. Signing made into Ortho Roy for the Coy. Main PLACE, G.S.O. 2 4 Platoons fine. G.S.O. 1, 36 Div.	

WAR DIARY
INTELLIGENCE SUMMARY

Army Form C. 2118

Sheet 41.

Place	Date	Hour	Summary of Events and Information	Remarks and references to Appendices
LESTREM	Apr 7.		Raining. Re-handed over the Canteen at LESTREM which we had been running for 30 or so days - from 38th Dn to 3y 6 Dn. Visit from Capt HATTRICK formerly RQMR Coy - now OC 21st Div Coy.	
	" 8		Fine cold. N. wind. Drill lecture, field etc. Cycle during Ans hut fny. Corpl HAZELL (O.Room) 10th on leave.	
	" 9		2nd Cold. Work as usual. Also on reclamation of Bure NEUVE CHAPELLE. Pte Fielding stands off strength - sent with 102 P.R.C.E.	
	" 10		Very fine & bright. Inspection of Billets. Night party as usual. Snow fire drawn 36 A + 3B.	
	" 11		Dull cold rain. Working parties at night. Inspection of men etc. As usual. Secret message re move on 20th.	
	" 12		Dull cold. Work and duties on account of rain - night party cancelled.	
	" 13		Bright high N wind. Work as usual. Secret march table. Officers for advance from Briq & Cadres; leave stopped & all moves recalled. Meeting at ROUGE CROIX. Latrines inspected in line.	

WAR DIARY / INTELLIGENCE SUMMARY

Army Form C. 2118

Sheet A.2.

Place	Date	Hour	Summary of Events and Information	Remarks and references to Appendices
LESTREM	Oct 14		Cold, mist, rain. Cook house inspection. Our Fatigue at MERVILLE finishing our drainage work.	Finis
"	"15		Fine. Cold. Bn in training - Patrol work. A.P.M. re whist of his box. Lieut. TALBOT to ST. VENANT re billets. Boots from the 4th midshown.	Finis
"	"16		Fine. Inspection 8 Coy. by O.C. Played 3rd Div.C.C. at football. We won 6-1. Advance guard to ST. VENANT	Jam
ST.VENANT	"17		Wet Cold. Moved to ST. VENANT in rainy. Came billets 20 homendy. Lieut. MORRIS returned from leave. One arrested for drunkenness including Ch. Park again.	Jam
"	"18		Still wet cold. Billets arranged at CUHEM for move on 19th. The transfer seemed all changed.	Jam
CUHEM	"19		Moved to CUHEM at 9am. Division in rest for severe training. Schone of training required for a fortnight. Arrangements for playing Lille match before moving to join 3rd Div. All Ranks specifically employed recalled.	Jam
	"20		Inter.Clar. Inspection by G.O.C. Major General Briggs, at FRESSIN (Sheet 11 LENS 1/100000)	Paul

1875 Wt. W 593/826 1,000,000 4/15 J.B.C. & A. A.D.S.S./Forms/C. 2118.

Army Form C. 2118

WAR DIARY
INTELLIGENCE SUMMARY

(Erase heading not required.)

Sheet 43.

Place	Date 1916	Hour	Summary of Events and Information	Remarks and references to Appendices
FRESSIN	April 21		Again moved to FRESSIN - near AZINCOURT - fine & clear. about 25 miles march. reported to B.M. Cav. Div. for training with Yeo. Brigade (Bgr of Div Cav). Transport arrived very late. - long hilly journey any fine country & hills.	
"	" 22		Bre warm. Lecture by 60.e. 3rd Cavalry Divn on Cavalry notes. Our new Created good impression on the inhabitants.	
"	" 23		Very fine. Inspection of man rifles etc. at Camp arrangements completed & O.M.S. running a good Canteen. Lecture on Reports	
"	" 24		Very fine. Staff ride. Officers MSS for work on Reporting on FRUGES - HESDIN Road. Training under two Staff Captains of 3rd Cav Div & farm.	
"	" 25		Very fine. Staff ride - Advance Guards. - work followed by Lecture farm. reports. issue of local maps.	
"	" 26		Very fair. Mur. of. Squadron out on Advance Guard rearie all day, fine. full inspection of hts.	
"	" 27		Very fine. Sqn out again in patrols as Vanguards with Cavalry all day farm.	

Army Form C. 2118

WAR DIARY
INTELLIGENCE SUMMARY
(Erase heading not required.)

Sheet 44

Place	Date 1916	Hour	Summary of Events and Information	Remarks and references to Appendices
ABSSIN	Ap 28		Fine. Advance guard to FRUHES then Cycle b open retirement in a Rear Guard action. out all day with Coy. 2 Lieut. MAIR & 2/Lt. THOMPSON join as reinforcement & replace Cpl. J. SMITH & Lieut. KNOTT. Ruffness much Andy. difficulty in finding Cpl. & own tr.	
"	29		Fine. Cavalry only at work to day. Cycles cleaned & men rifles inspected by own.	
"	30		Fine. Coy. had out ratioted Canteen having well - propose to PRI a little delay in delivery of food owing to our moves.	

www.ingramcontent.com/pod-product-compliance
Lightning Source LLC
Chambersburg PA
CBHW081359160426
43193CB00013B/2069